Contents

A Note from the Author

KYAA, FOR SOME REASON, I WAS ASKED TO DO A ROMANCE
STORY. HALFWAY THROUGH, I REALLY STARTED TO REGRET
IT. I'M JUST NO GOOD AT WRITING ROMANCE. I REALLY
WORRIED ABOUT HOW TO RESOLVE THE STORY, AND WELL...
THIS IS WHAT I ENDED UP WITH. WHAT ON EARTH WILL
HAPPEN TO SUNAKO NEXT? I HOPE YOU'LL STICK AROUND
AND FIND OUT.

—Tomoko Hayakawa

Honorifics Explained

Throughout the Del Rey Manga books, you will find Japanese honorifics left intact in the translations. For those not familiar with how the Japanese use honorifics and, more important, how they differ from American honorifics, we present this brief overview.

Politeness has always been a critical facet of Japanese culture. Ever since the feudal era, when Japan was a highly stratified society, use of honorifics—which can be defined as polite speech that indicates relationship or status—has played an essential role in the Japanese language. When addressing someone in Japanese, an honorific usually takes the form of a suffix attached to one's name (example: "Asuna-san"), is used as a title at the end of one's name, or appears in place of the name itself (example: "Negi-sensei," or simply "Sensei!").

Honorifics can be expressions of respect or endearment. In the context of manga and anime, honorifics give insight into the nature of the relationship between characters. Many English translations leave out these important honorifics and therefore distort the feel of the original Japanese. Because Japanese honorifics contain nuances that English honorifics lack, it is our policy at Del Rey not to translate them. Here, instead, is a guide to some of the honorifics you may encounter in Del Rey Manga.

-san: This is the most common honorific and is equivalent to Mr., Miss, Ms., or Mrs. It is the all-purpose honorific and can be used in any situation where politeness is required.

-sama: This is one level higher than "-san" and is used to confer great respect.

-dono: This comes from the word "tono," which means "lord." It is an even higher level than "-sama" and confers utmost respect.

-kun: This suffix is used at the end of boys' names to express famil-
iarity or endearment. It is also sometimes used by men among
friends, or when addressing someone younger or of a lower
station.

-chan: This is used to express endearment, mostly toward girls. It is
also used for little boys, pets, and even among lovers. It gives
a sense of childish cuteness.

Bozu: This is an informal way to refer to a boy, similar to the English
terms "kid" and "squirt."

**Sempai/
Senpai:** This title suggests that the addressee is one's senior in a group
or organization. It is most often used in a school setting, where
underclassmen refer to their upperclassmen as "sempai." It
can also be used in the workplace, such as when a newer employee addresses an employee who has seniority in the com-
pany.

Kohai: This is the opposite of "sempai" and is used toward underclassmen in school or newcomers in the workplace. It connotes
that the addressee is of a lower station.

Sensei: Literally meaning "one who has come before," this title is used
for teachers, doctors, or masters of any profession or art.

-[blank]: This is usually forgotten in these lists, but it is perhaps the
most significant difference between Japanese and English. The
lack of honorific means that the speaker has permission to ad-
dress the person in a very intimate way. Usually, only family,
spouses, or very close friends have this kind of permission.
Known as *yobisute*, it can be gratifying when someone who
has earned the intimacy starts to call one by one's name without an honorific. But when that intimacy hasn't been earned,
it can be very insulting.

THE wallflower

YAMATONADESHIKO SHICHIHENGE

ヤマトナデシコ七変化♡

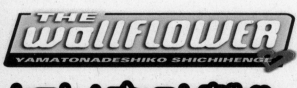

CONTENTS

WALLFLOWER'S BEAUTIFUL CAST OF CHARACTERS (?)

SUNAKO NAKAHARA
KYOHEI TAKANO— A STRONG FIGHTER, "I'M THE KING"
TAKENAGA ODA— A CARING FEMINIST
RANMARU MORII— A TRUE LADY'S MAN
YUKINOJO TOYAMA— A GENTLE, CHEERFUL, AND VERY EMOTIONAL GUY

SUNAKO IS A DARK LONER WHO LOVES HORROR MOVIES. WHEN HER AUNT, THE LANDLADY OF A BOARDINGHOUSE, LEAVES TOWN WITH HER BOYFRIEND, SUNAKO IS FORCED TO LIVE WITH FOUR HANDSOME GUYS. SUNAKO'S AUNT MAKES A DEAL WITH THE BOYS, WHICH CAUSES NOTHING BUT HEADACHES FOR SUNAKO. "MAKE SUNAKO INTO A LADY, AND YOU CAN LIVE RENT-FREE FOR THREE YEARS. THE GUYS ARE NOWHERE NEAR TURNING SUNAKO INTO A LADY AND HER RELATIONSHIP WITH KYOHEI ISN'T PROGRESSING AT ALL. THEN AGAIN, IN THE LAST VOLUME, THEY DID BOTH DRAW THE SAME "LUCK IN LOVE" FORTUNE...

Chapter 83 Special Bonus Manga – Come Back, Machiko!

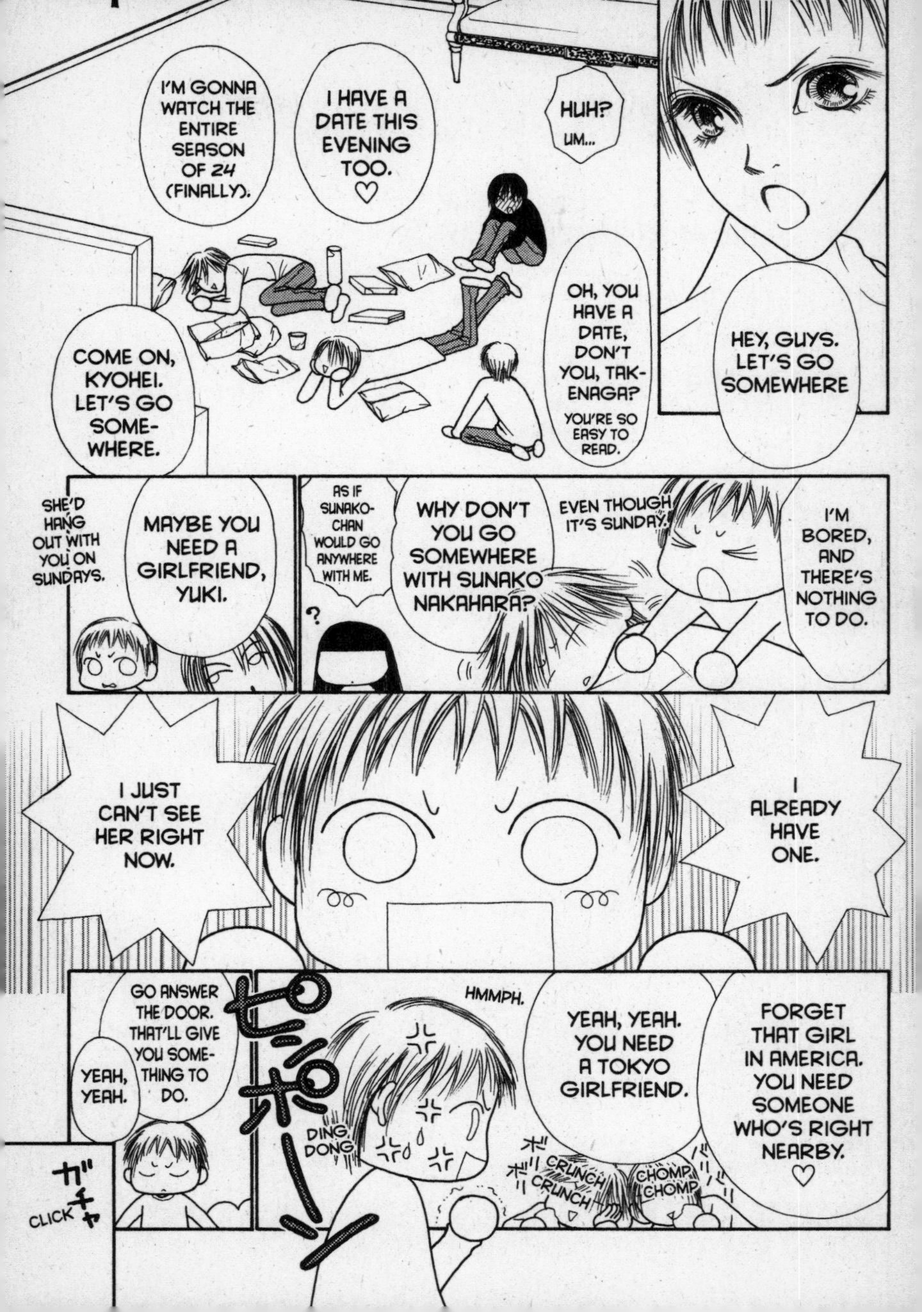

HEY, GUYS. LET'S GO SOMEWHERE
HUH? UM...
I HAVE A DATE THIS EVENING TOO. ♡
I'M GONNA WATCH THE ENTIRE SEASON OF 24 (FINALLY).
OH, YOU HAVE A DATE, DON'T YOU, TAKENAGA?
YOU'RE SO EASY TO READ.
COME ON, KYOHEI. LET'S GO SOMEWHERE.
I'M BORED, AND THERE'S NOTHING TO DO.
EVEN THOUGH IT'S SUNDAY.
WHY DON'T YOU GO SOMEWHERE WITH SUNAKO NAKAHARA?
AS IF SUNAKO-CHAN WOULD GO ANYWHERE WITH ME.
?
MAYBE YOU NEED A GIRLFRIEND, YUKI.
SHE'D HANG OUT WITH YOU ON SUNDAYS.
I ALREADY HAVE ONE.
I JUST CAN'T SEE HER RIGHT NOW.
FORGET THAT GIRL IN AMERICA. YOU NEED SOMEONE WHO'S RIGHT NEARBY. ♡
YEAH, YEAH. YOU NEED A TOKYO GIRLFRIEND.
HMMPH.
バリバリ
CHOMP CHOMP
ボリボリ
CRUNCH CRUNCH
ピンポーン
DING DONG
GO ANSWER THE DOOR. THAT'LL GIVE YOU SOMETHING TO DO.
YEAH, YEAH.
ガチャ
CLICK

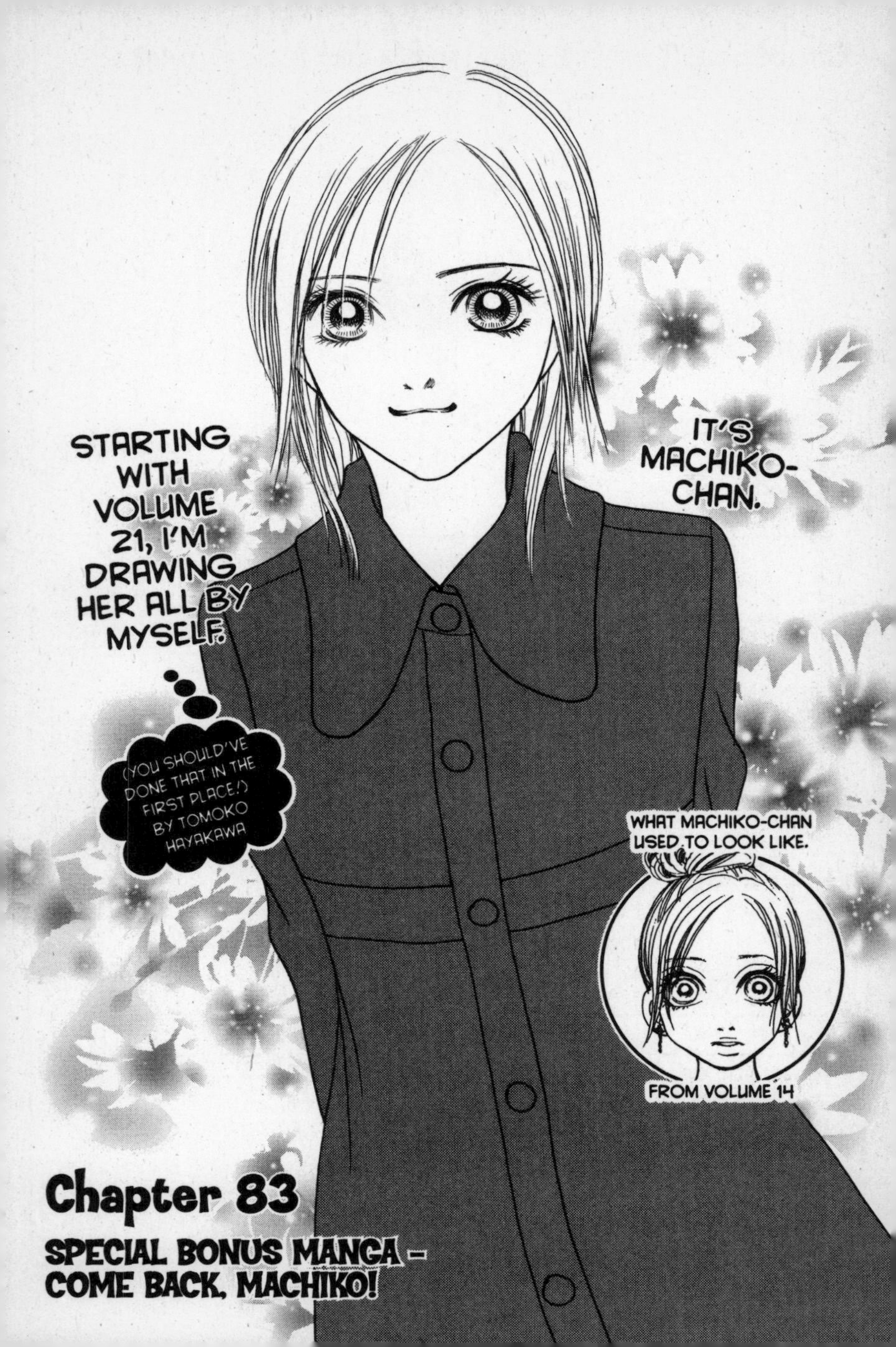
IT'S MACHIKO-CHAN.
STARTING WITH VOLUME 21, I'M DRAWING HER ALL BY MYSELF.
(YOU SHOULD'VE DONE THAT IN THE FIRST PLACE!) BY TOMOKO HAYAKAWA
WHAT MACHIKO-CHAN USED TO LOOK LIKE.
FROM VOLUME 14

Chapter 83

SPECIAL BONUS MANGA - COME BACK, MACHIKO!

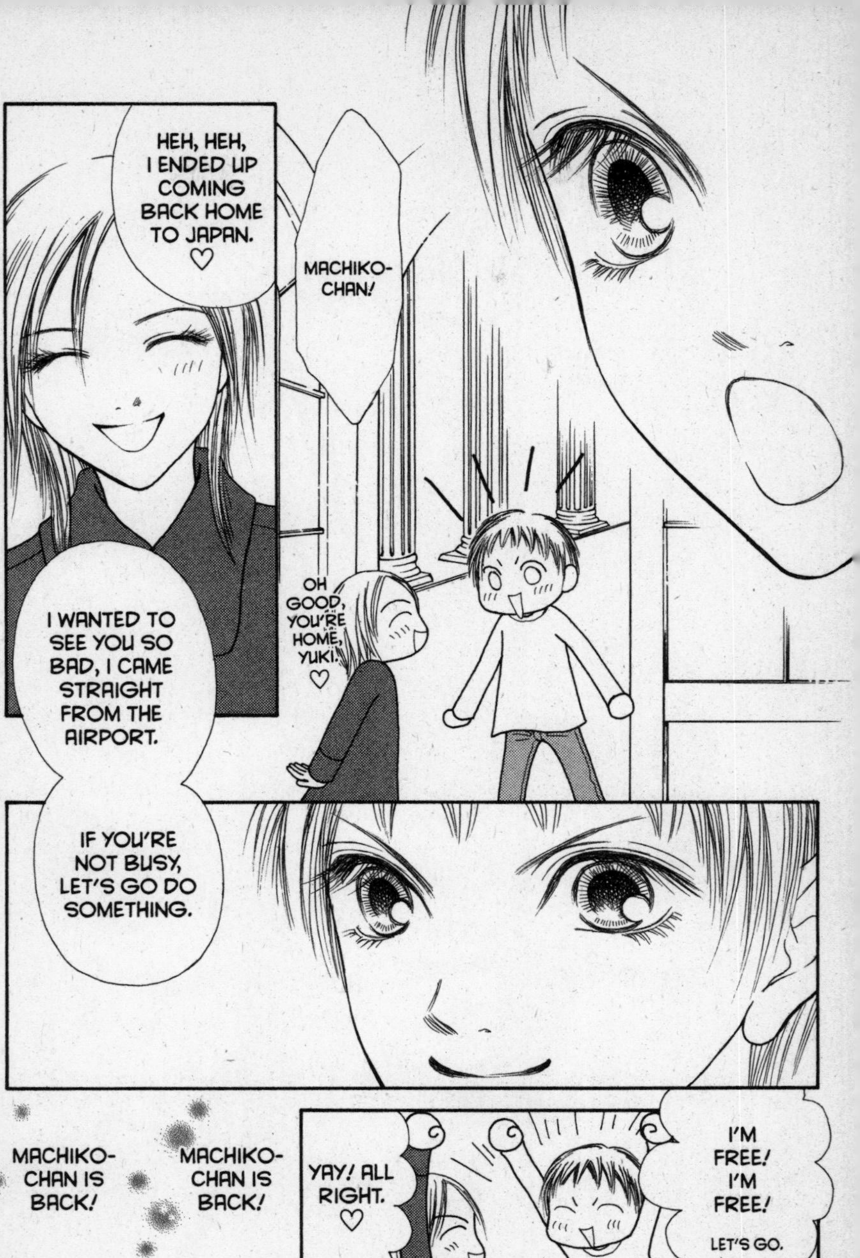
MACHIKO-CHAN!
OH GOOD, YOU'RE HOME, YUKI. ♡
HEH, HEH, I ENDED UP COMING BACK HOME TO JAPAN. ♡
I WANTED TO SEE YOU SO BAD, I CAME STRAIGHT FROM THE AIRPORT.
IF YOU'RE NOT BUSY, LET'S GO DO SOMETHING.
I'M FREE! I'M FREE!
LET'S GO.
YAY! ALL RIGHT. ♡
MACHIKO-CHAN IS BACK!
MACHIKO-CHAN IS BACK!

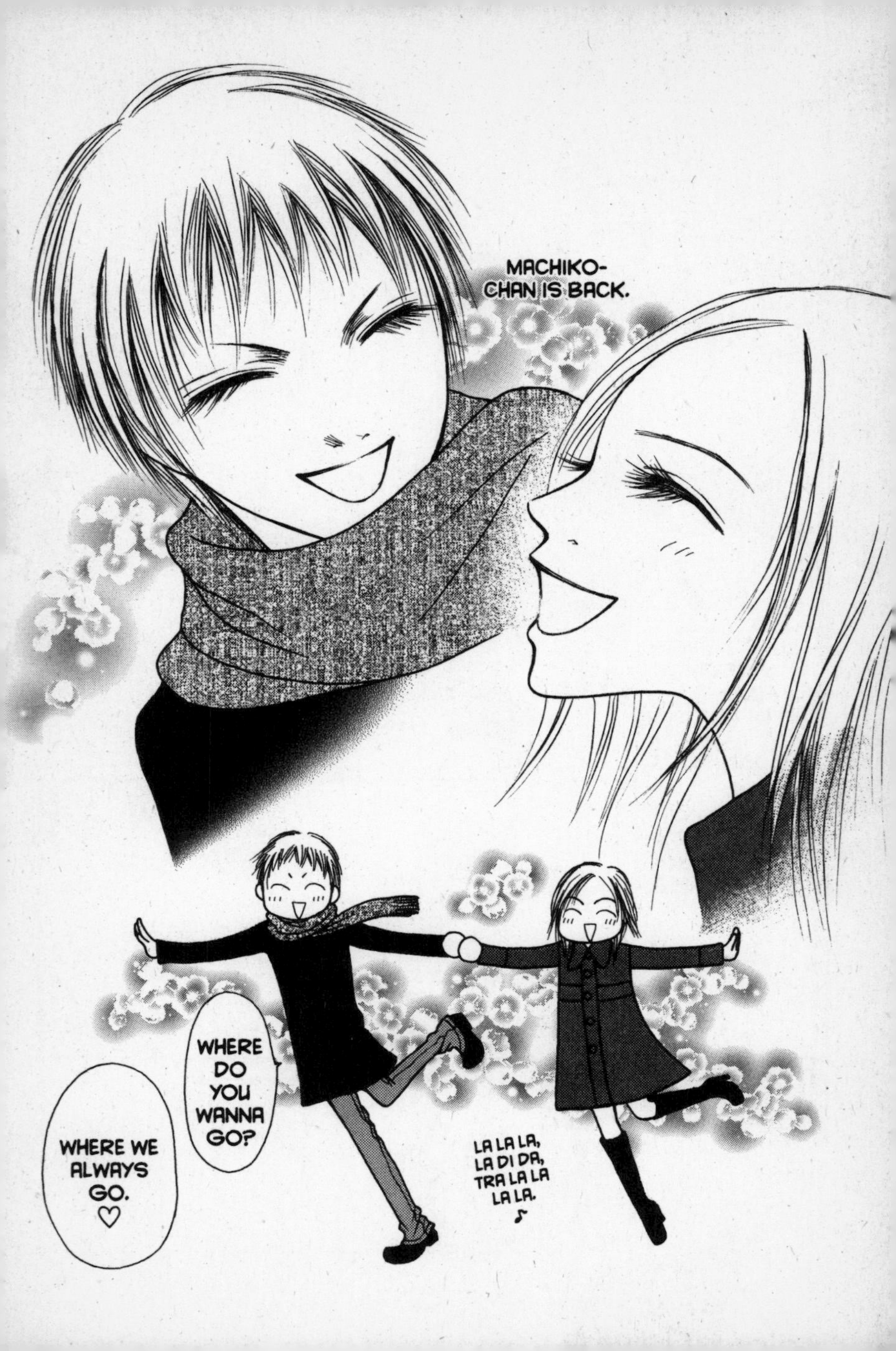
MACHIKO-CHAN IS BACK.
LA LA LA, LA DI DA, TRA LA LA LA LA. ♪
WHERE DO YOU WANNA GO?
WHERE WE ALWAYS GO. ♡

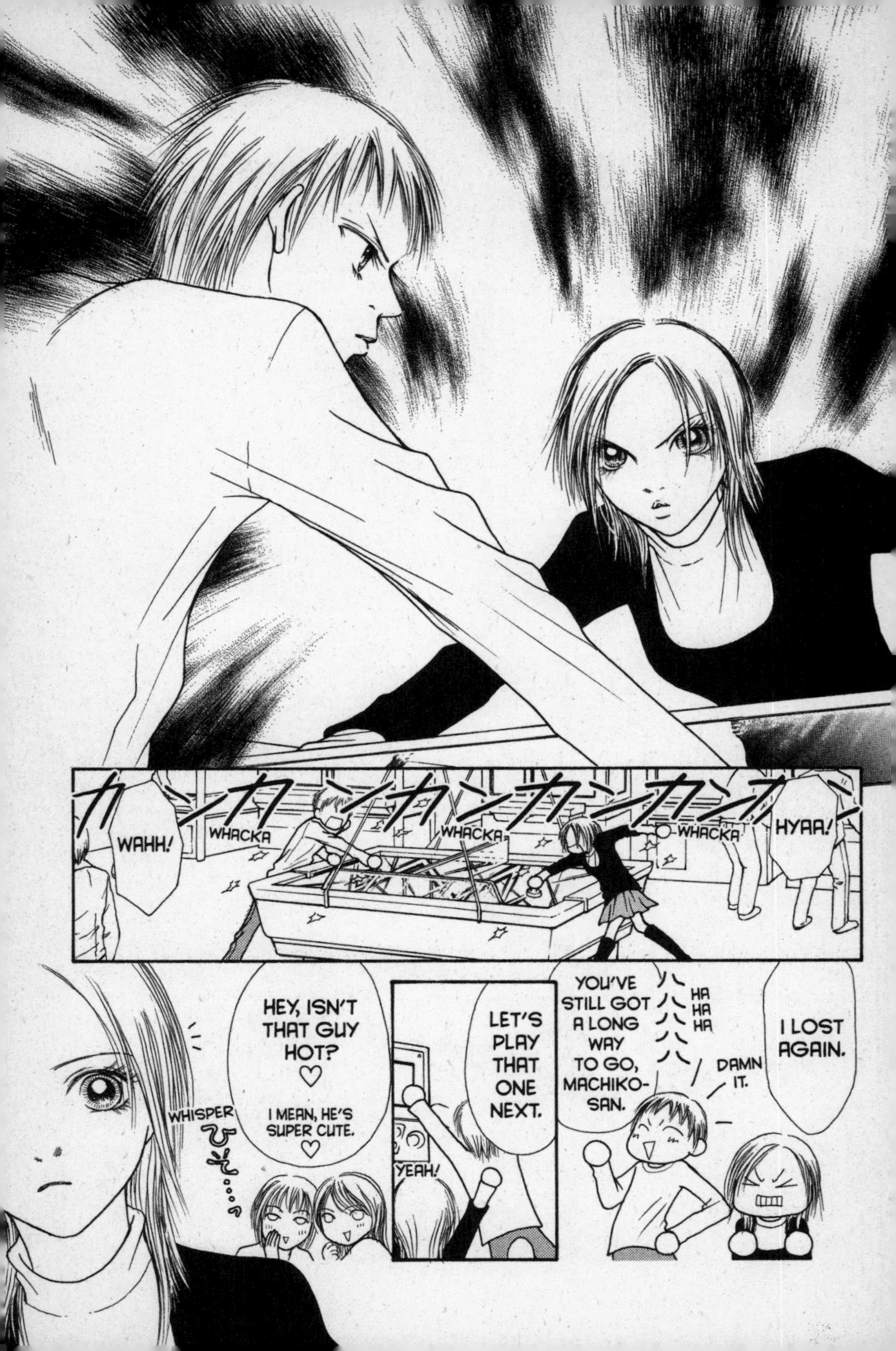

カンカンカンカンカン
HYAA!
WHACKA
WHACKA
WHACKA
WAHH!
I LOST AGAIN.
DAMN IT.
HA HA HA
YOU'VE STILL GOT A LONG WAY TO GO, MACHIKO-SAN.
LET'S PLAY THAT ONE NEXT.
YEAH!
HEY, ISN'T THAT GUY HOT? ♡
I MEAN, HE'S SUPER CUTE. ♡
WHISPER

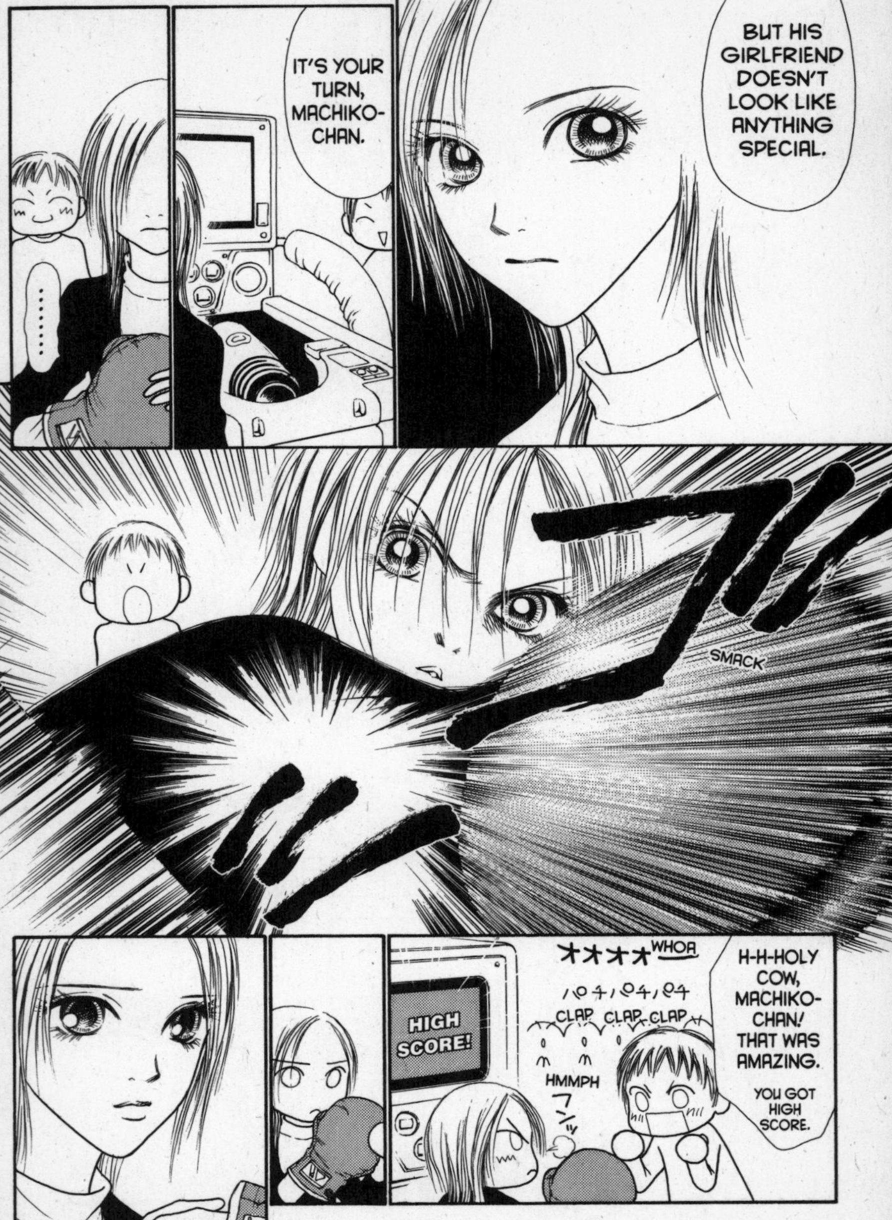
BUT HIS GIRLFRIEND DOESN'T LOOK LIKE ANYTHING SPECIAL.
IT'S YOUR TURN, MACHIKO-CHAN.
......
SMACK
H-H-HOLY COW, MACHIKO-CHAN! THAT WAS AMAZING.
オオオオ WHOA
パチパチパチ CLAP CLAP CLAP
HIGH SCORE!
YOU GOT HIGH SCORE.
HMMPH フンッ

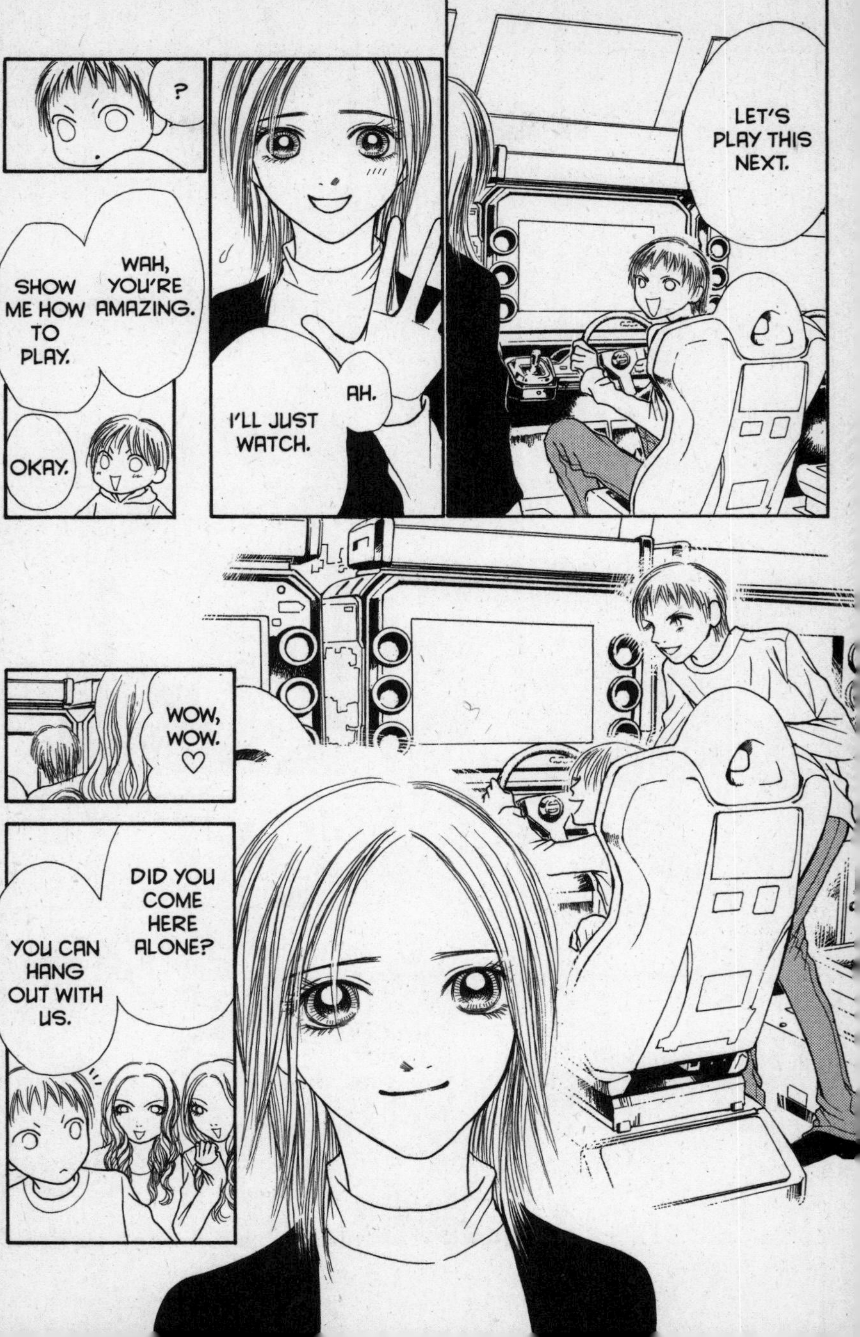
LET'S PLAY THIS NEXT.
AH.
I'LL JUST WATCH.
?
WAH, YOU'RE AMAZING.
SHOW ME HOW TO PLAY.
OKAY.
WOW, WOW. ♡
DID YOU COME HERE ALONE?
YOU CAN HANG OUT WITH US.

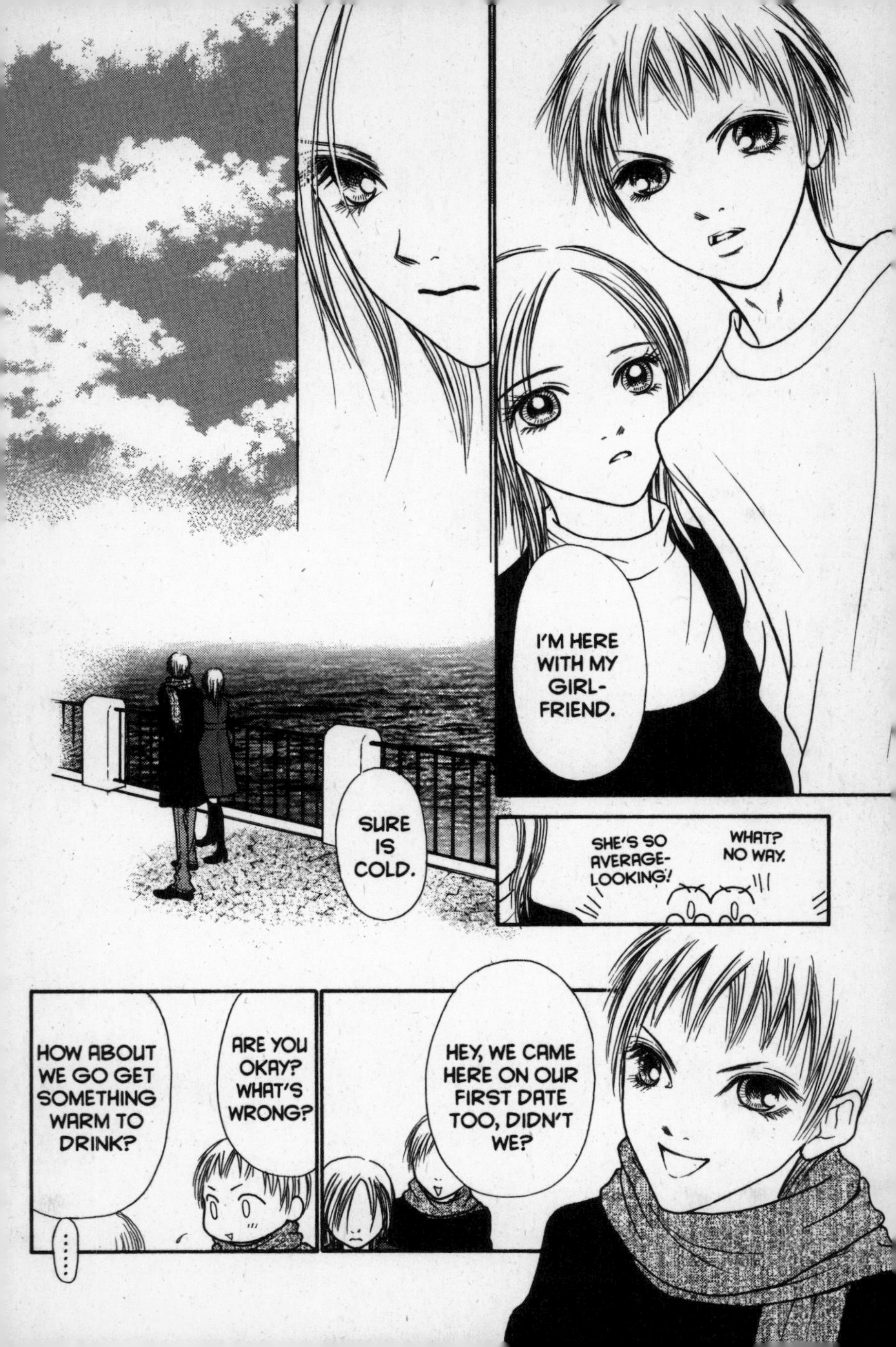
I'M HERE WITH MY GIRL-FRIEND.
WHAT? NO WAY.
SHE'S SO AVERAGE-LOOKING!
SURE IS COLD.
HEY, WE CAME HERE ON OUR FIRST DATE TOO, DIDN'T WE?
ARE YOU OKAY? WHAT'S WRONG?
HOW ABOUT WE GO GET SOMETHING WARM TO DRINK?
......

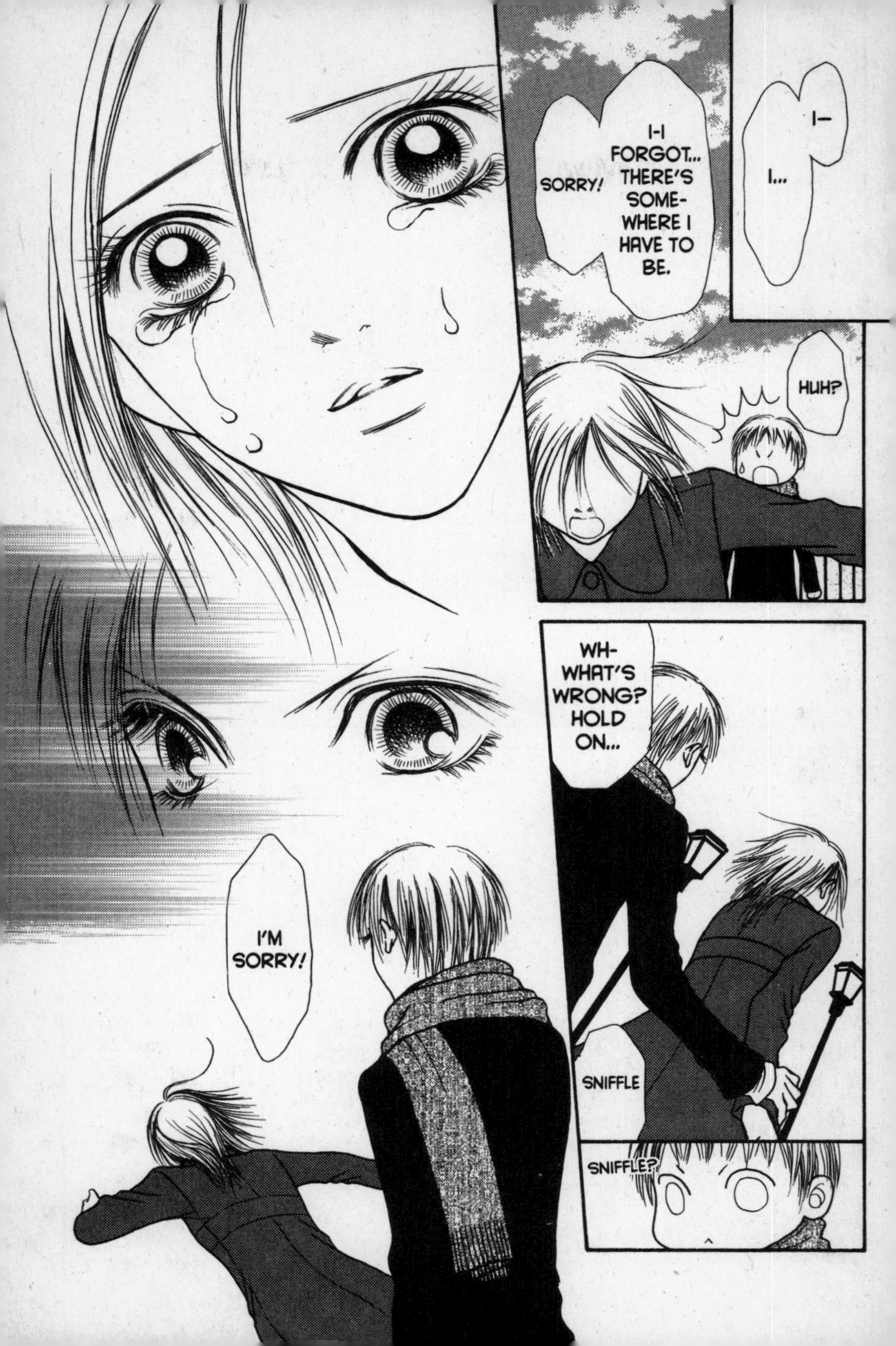

I—
I...
I-I FORGOT... THERE'S SOME-WHERE I HAVE TO BE.
SORRY!
HUH?
WH-WHAT'S WRONG? HOLD ON...
SNIFFLE
SNIFFLE?
I'M SORRY!

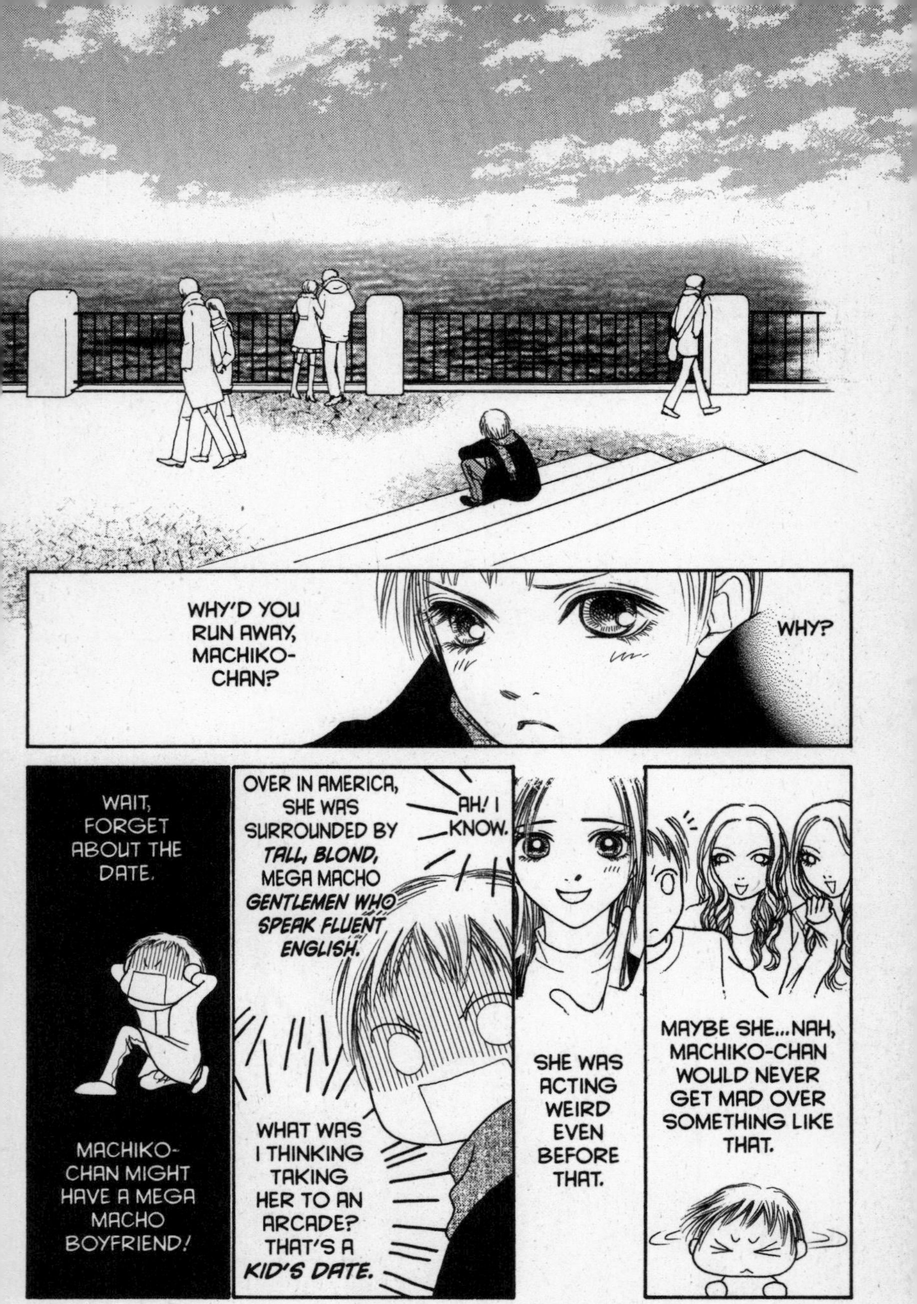
WHY?
WHY'D YOU RUN AWAY, MACHIKO-CHAN?
MAYBE SHE...NAH, MACHIKO-CHAN WOULD NEVER GET MAD OVER SOMETHING LIKE THAT.
SHE WAS ACTING WEIRD EVEN BEFORE THAT.
AH! I KNOW.
OVER IN AMERICA, SHE WAS SURROUNDED BY *TALL, BLOND,* MEGA MACHO *GENTLEMEN WHO SPEAK FLUENT ENGLISH.*
WHAT WAS I THINKING TAKING HER TO AN ARCADE? THAT'S A *KID'S DATE.*
WAIT, FORGET ABOUT THE DATE.
MACHIKO-CHAN MIGHT HAVE A MEGA MACHO BOYFRIEND!

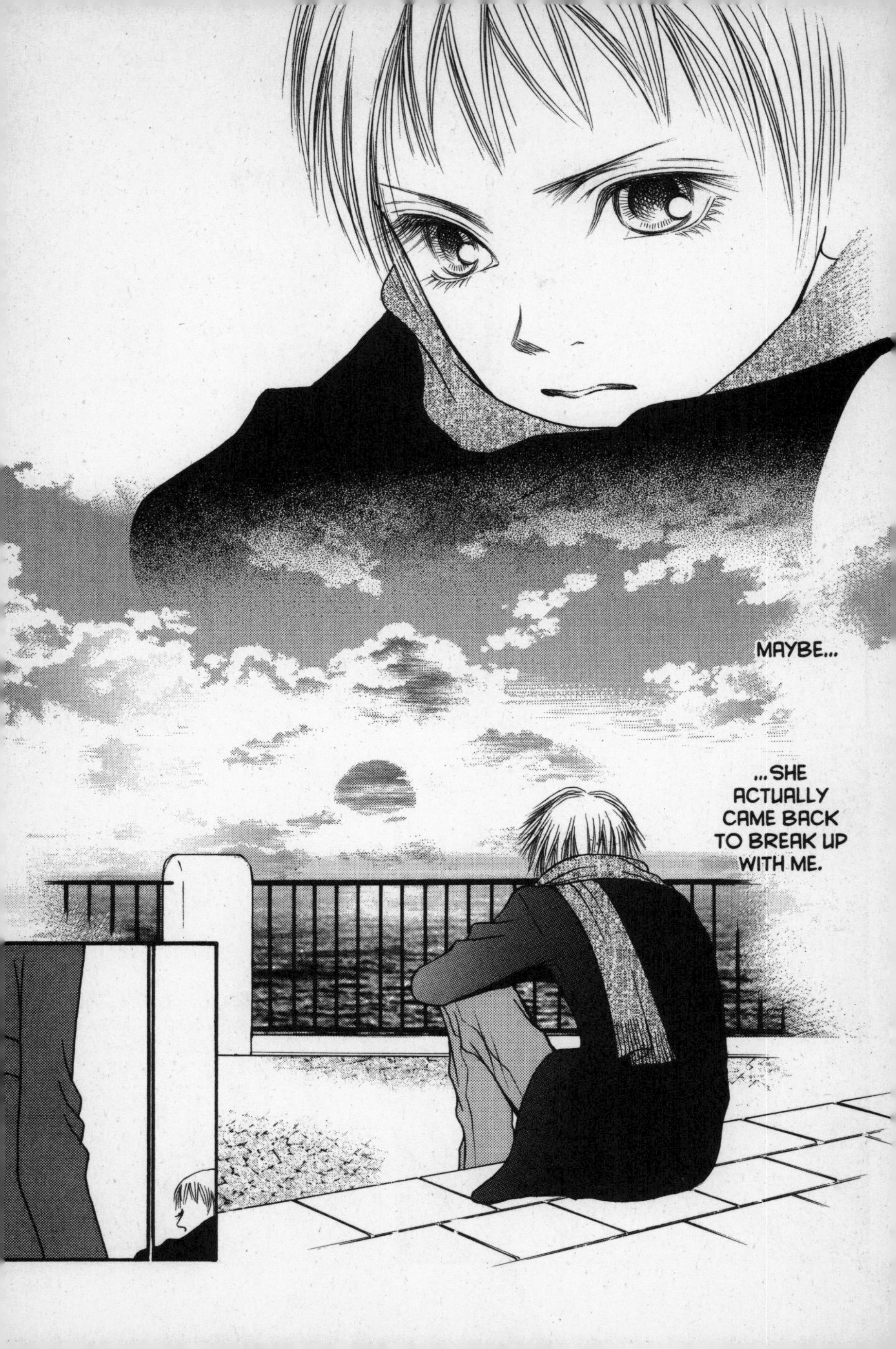
MAYBE...
...SHE ACTUALLY CAME BACK TO BREAK UP WITH ME.

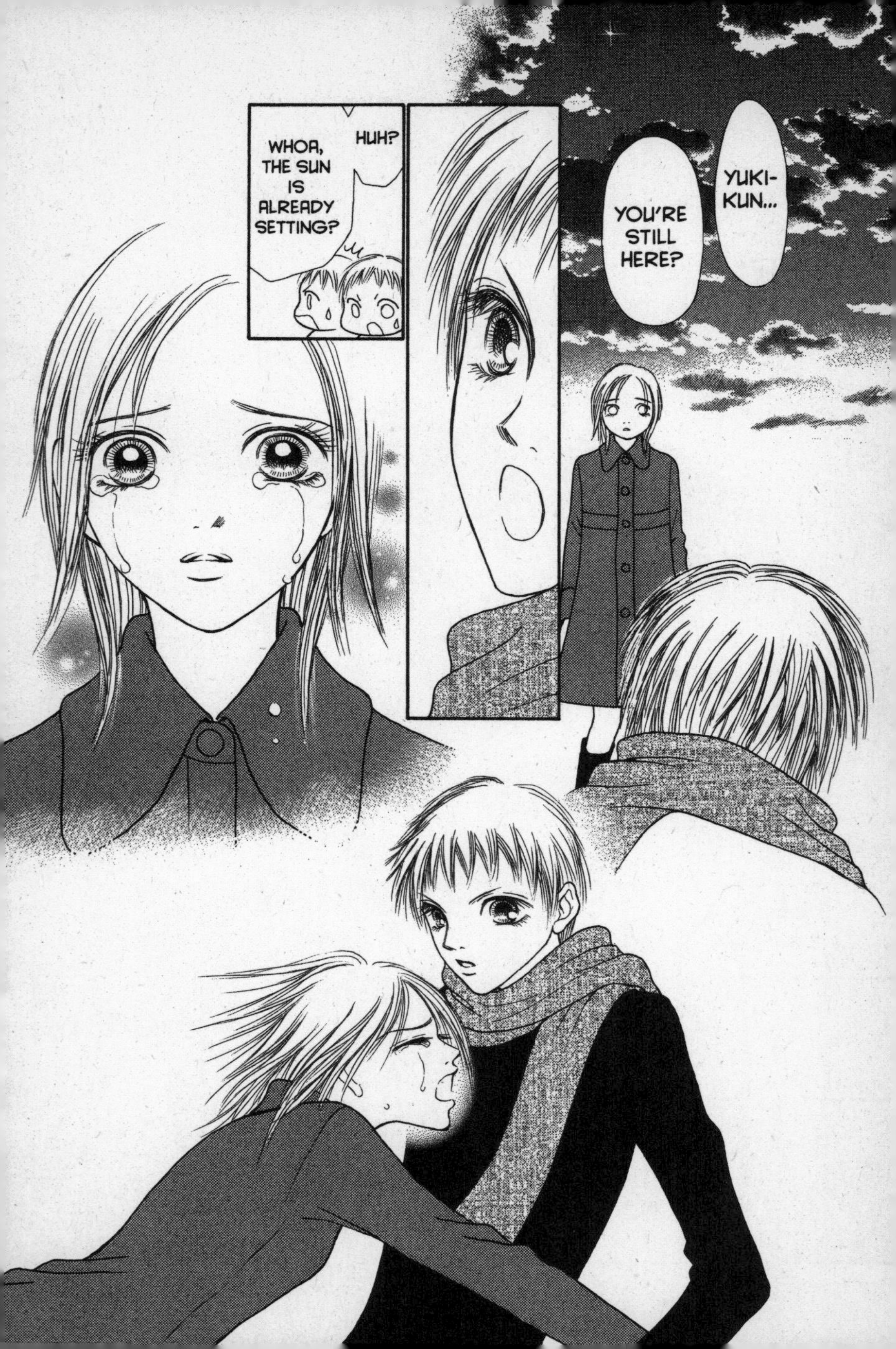
YUKI-KUN...
YOU'RE STILL HERE?
HUH?
WHOA, THE SUN IS ALREADY SETTING?

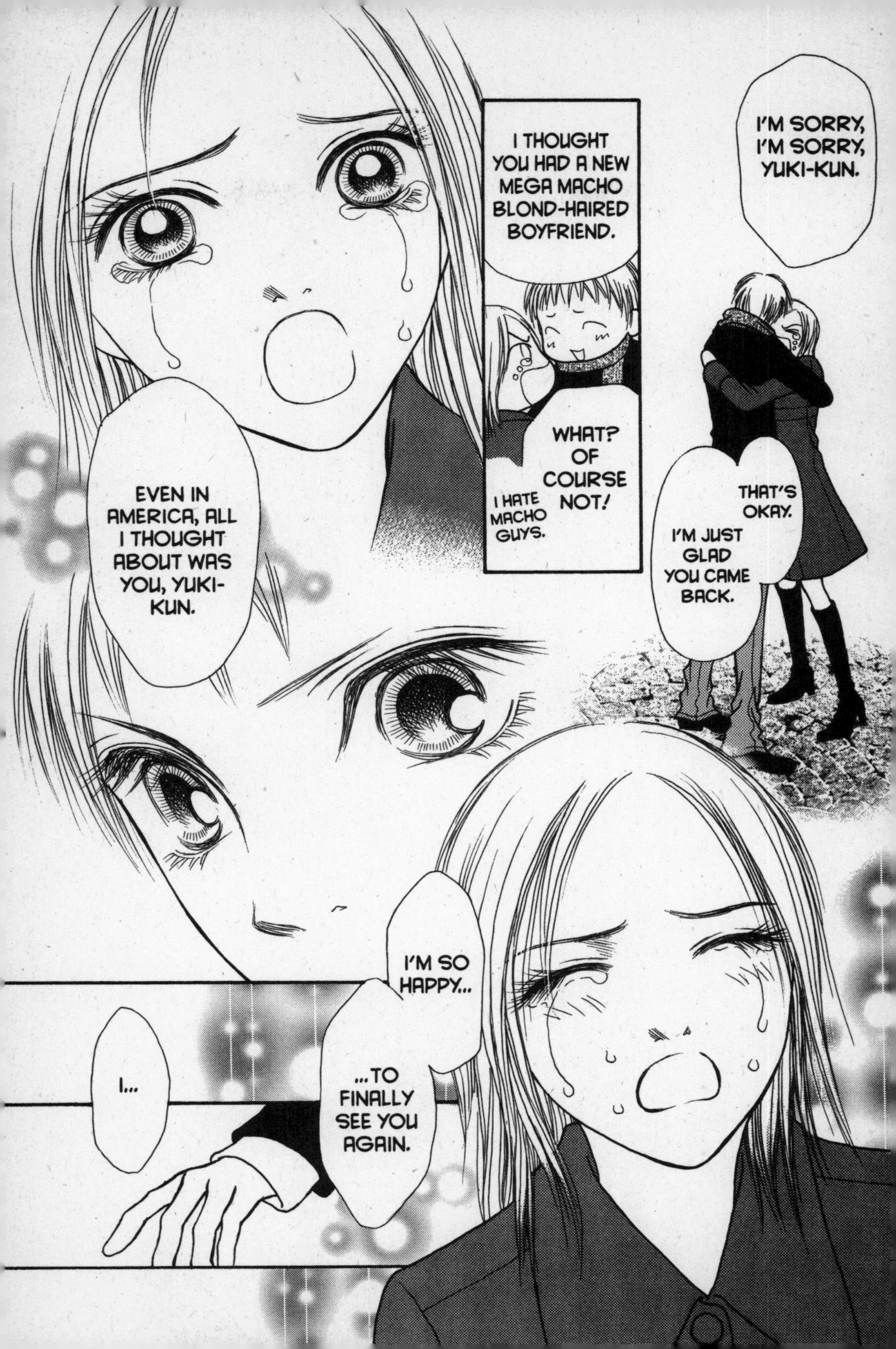
I'M SORRY, I'M SORRY, YUKI-KUN.
THAT'S OKAY.
I'M JUST GLAD YOU CAME BACK.
I THOUGHT YOU HAD A NEW MEGA MACHO BLOND-HAIRED BOYFRIEND.
WHAT? OF COURSE NOT!
I HATE MACHO GUYS.
EVEN IN AMERICA, ALL I THOUGHT ABOUT WAS YOU, YUKI-KUN.
I'M SO HAPPY...
...TO FINALLY SEE YOU AGAIN.
I...

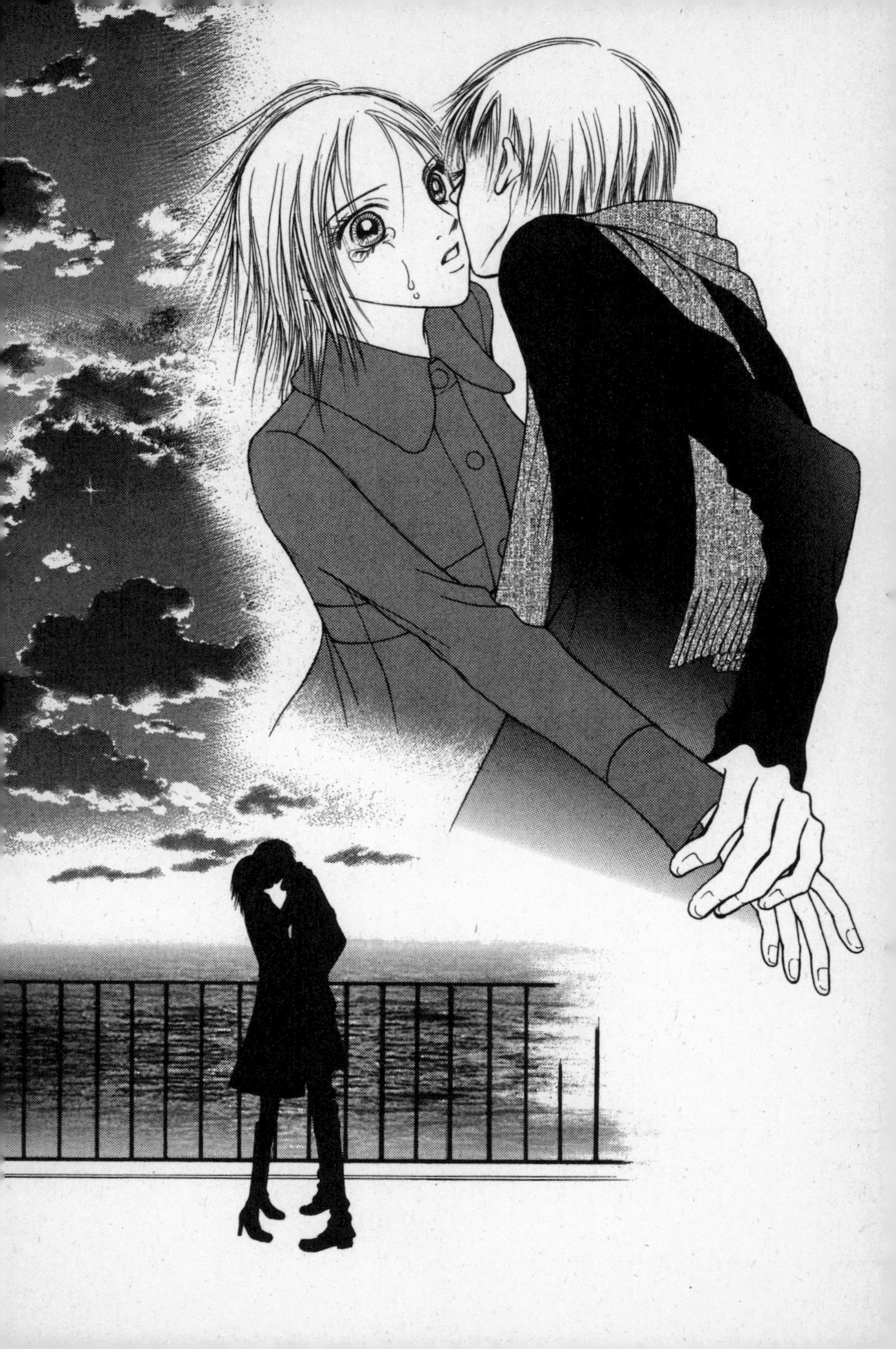

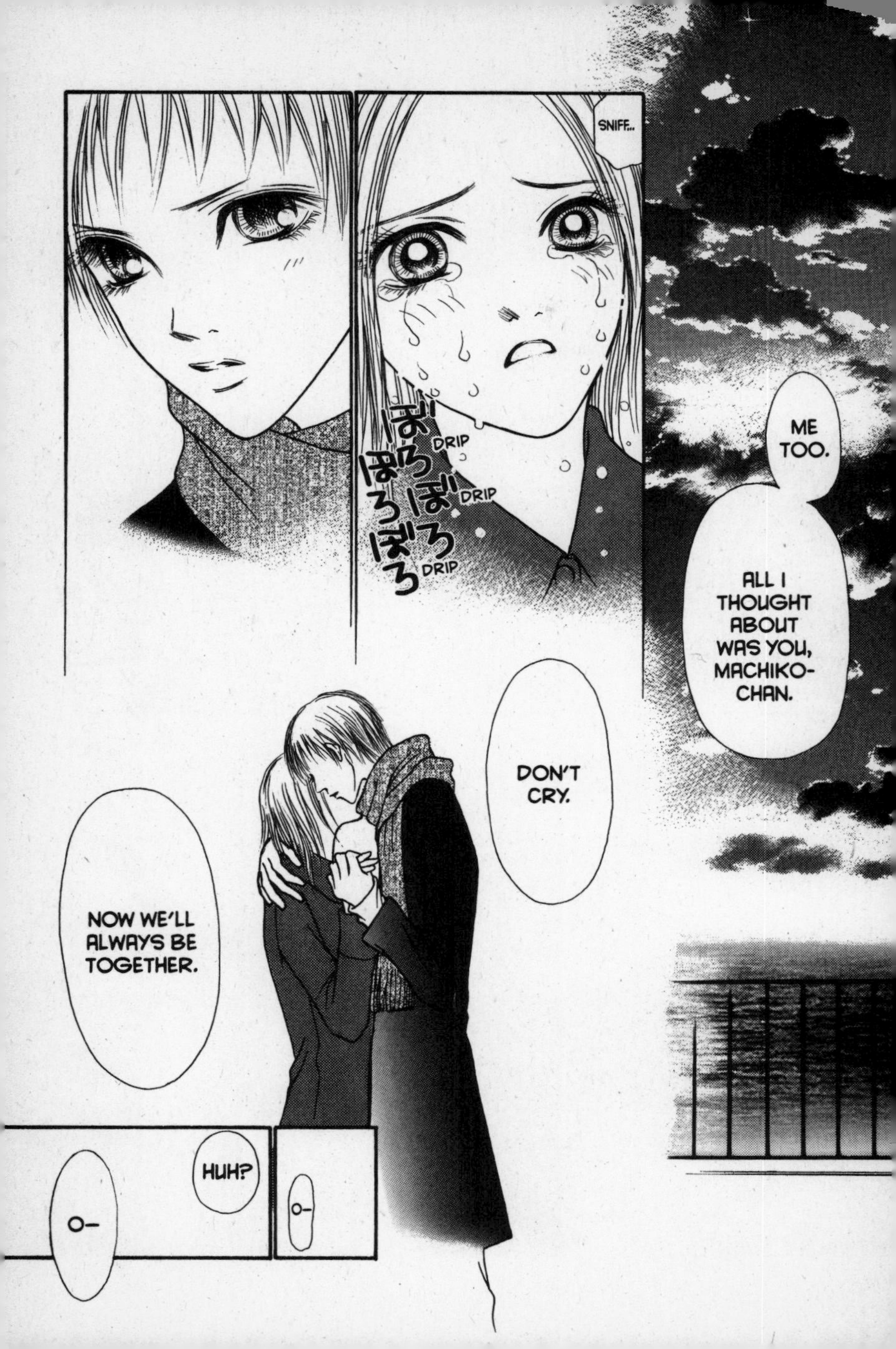
ME TOO.
ALL I THOUGHT ABOUT WAS YOU, MACHIKO-CHAN.
SNIFF...
ぽろぽろ
DRIP
ぽろぽろ
DRIP
ぽろぽろ
DRIP
DON'T CRY.
NOW WE'LL ALWAYS BE TOGETHER.
O–
HUH?
O–

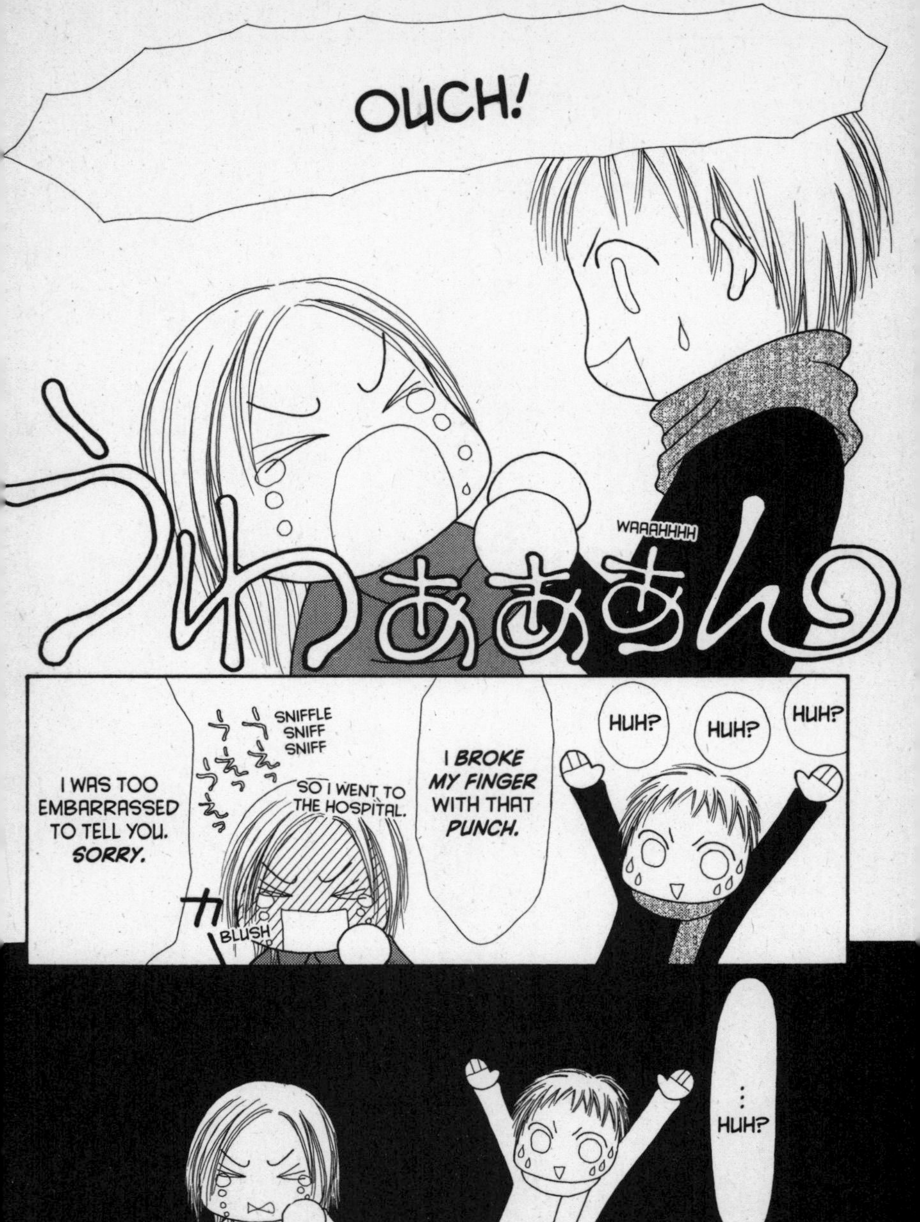
OUCH!
うわあああん
WAAAHHHH
HUH?
HUH?
HUH?
I BROKE MY FINGER WITH THAT PUNCH.
SO I WENT TO THE HOSPITAL.
SNIFFLE SNIFF SNIFF
I WAS TOO EMBARRASSED TO TELL YOU. SORRY.
BLUSH
... HUH?

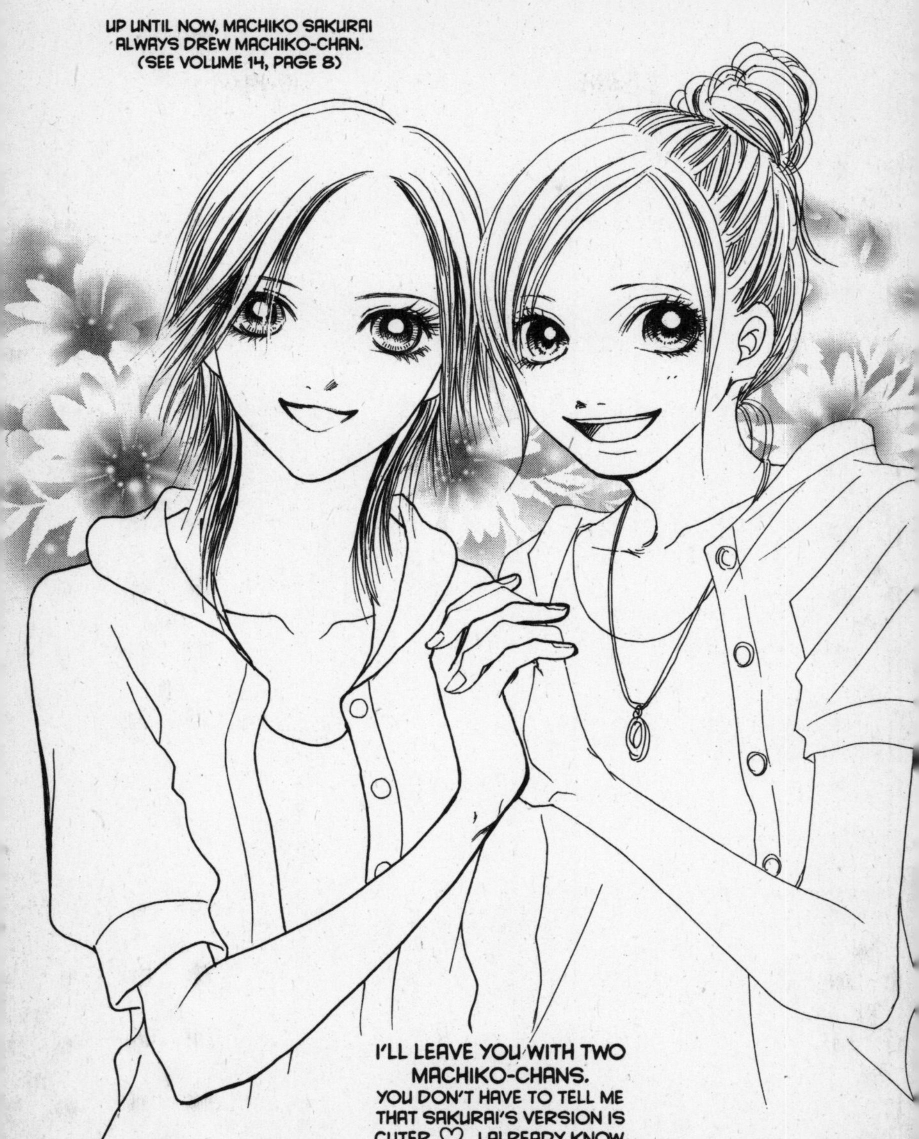
UP UNTIL NOW, MACHIKO SAKURAI ALWAYS DREW MACHIKO-CHAN. (SEE VOLUME 14, PAGE 8)
I'LL LEAVE YOU WITH TWO MACHIKO-CHANS.
YOU DON'T HAVE TO TELL ME THAT SAKURAI'S VERSION IS CUTER. ♡...I ALREADY KNOW.

Chapter 84

THE LEGEND OF KYOHEI BEGINS ANEW

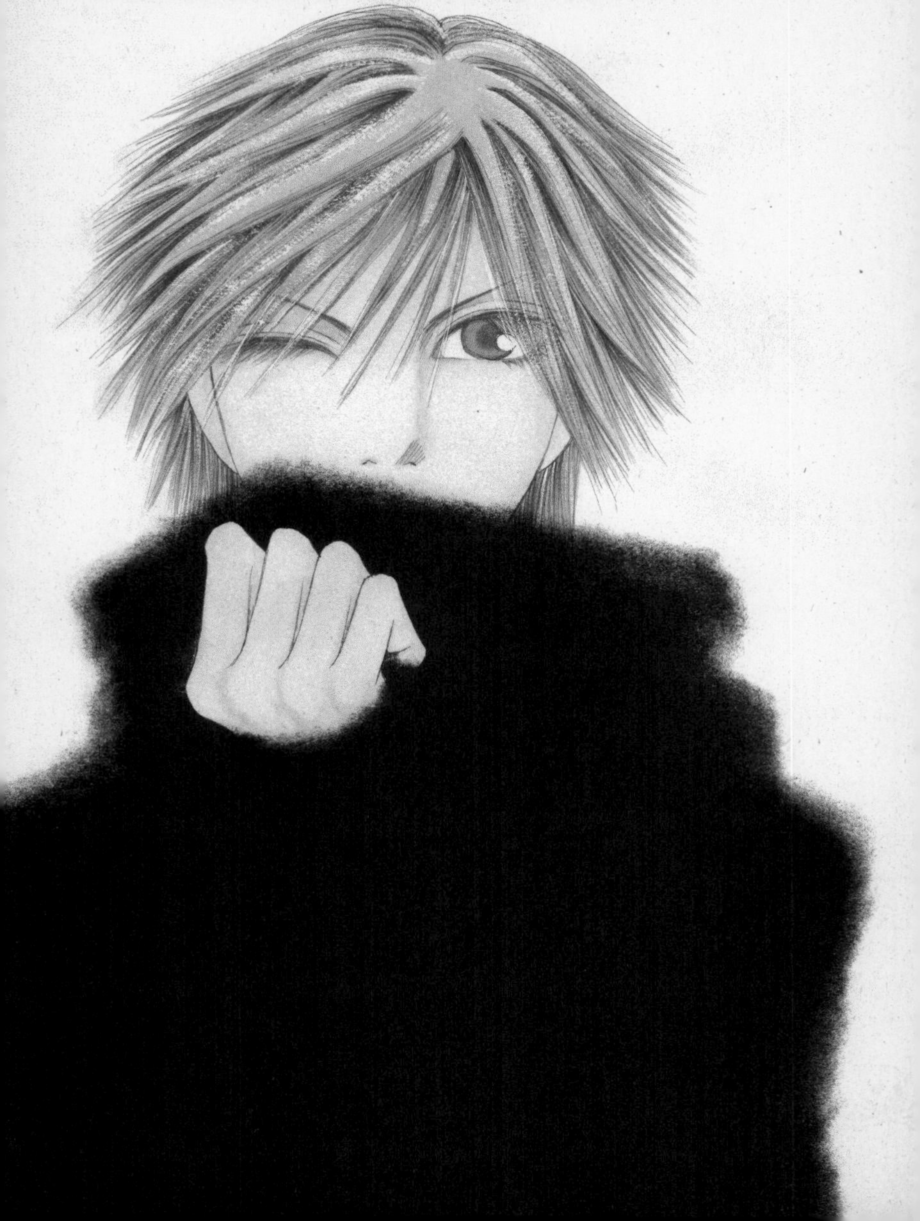

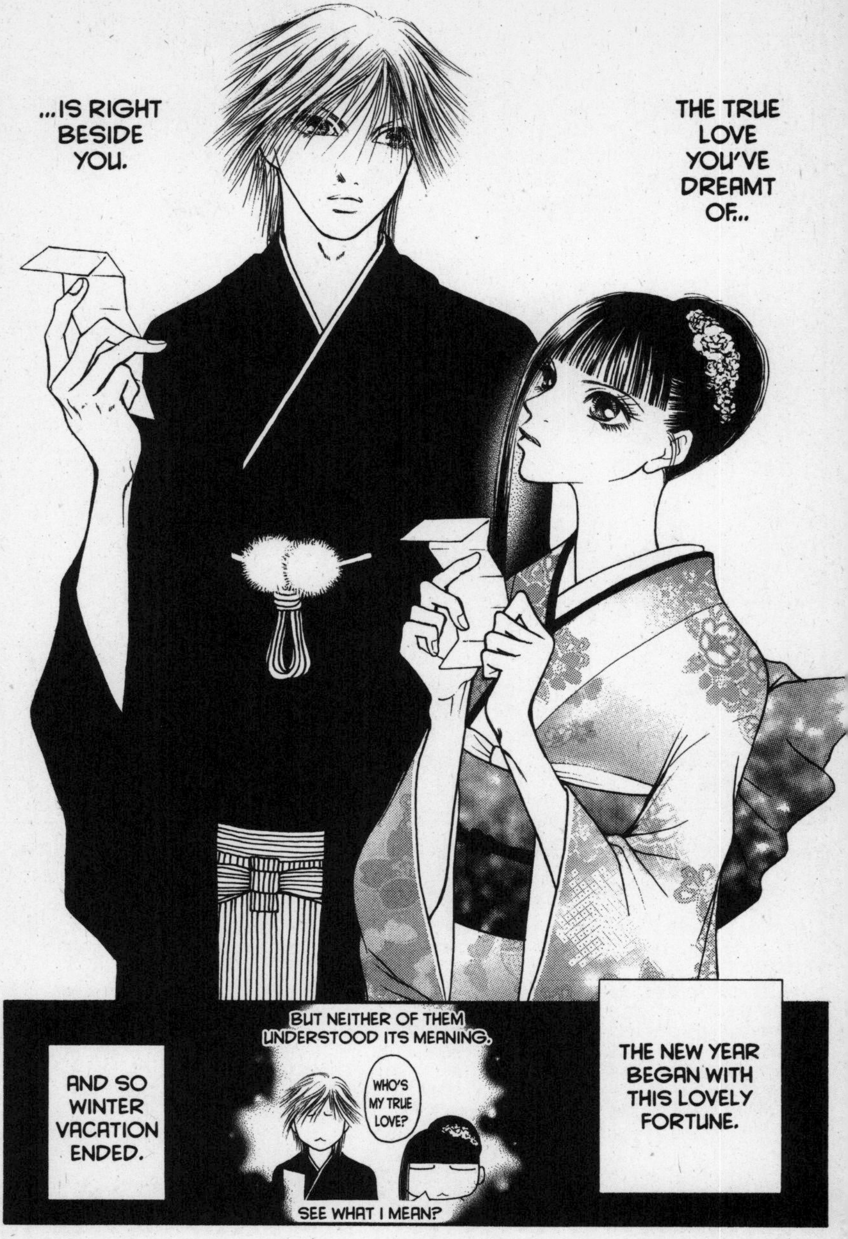
THE TRUE LOVE YOU'VE DREAMT OF...
...IS RIGHT BESIDE YOU.
THE NEW YEAR BEGAN WITH THIS LOVELY FORTUNE.
BUT NEITHER OF THEM UNDERSTOOD ITS MEANING.
WHO'S MY TRUE LOVE?
SEE WHAT I MEAN?
AND SO WINTER VACATION ENDED.

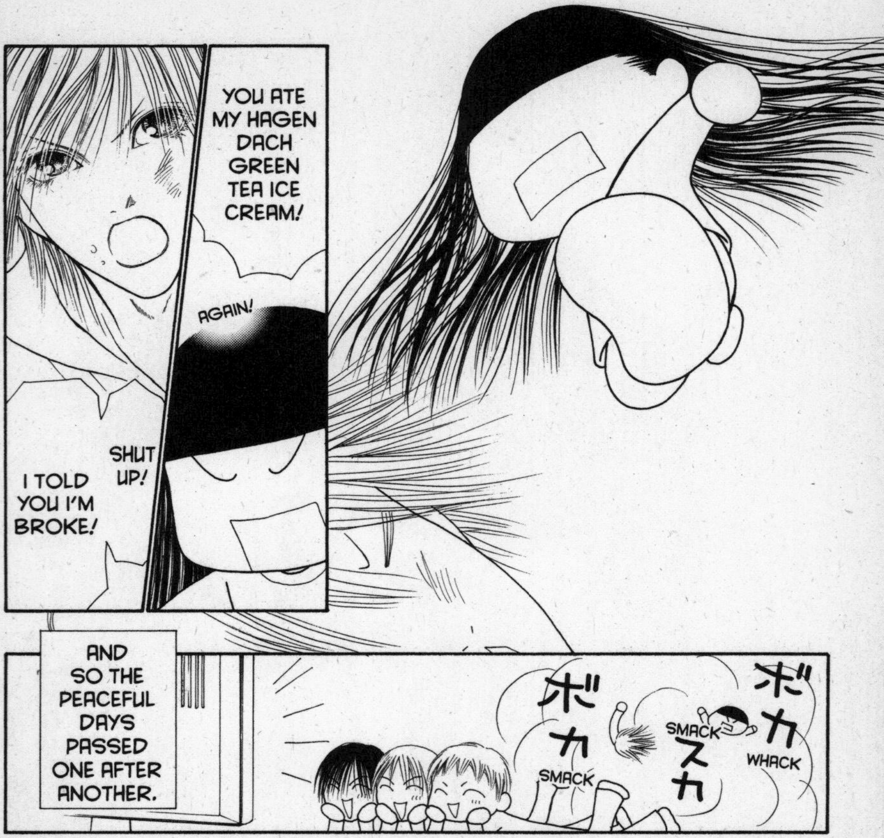
YOU ATE MY HAGEN DACH GREEN TEA ICE CREAM!
AGAIN!
SHUT UP!
I TOLD YOU I'M BROKE!
ボカ
WHACK
スカ
SMACK
ボカ
SMACK
AND SO THE PEACEFUL DAYS PASSED ONE AFTER ANOTHER.

BEHIND THE SCENES

THE TOUGH TIMES I TALKED ABOUT IN VOLUME 20 HAVEN'T ENDED YET, SO I'M JUST GONNA TALK ABOUT FUN STUFF. I WROTE THIS STORY IN DECEMBER. ♥ YEP, I WENT TO A LOT OF SHOWS THAT MONTH!

I WENT TO HOKKAIDO TO SEE MERRY ♥ AND KIYOHARU-SAMA. AFTER I TURNED IN THIS STORY, I WENT TO SEE NEW ROTE'KA, AND ON CHRISTMAS EVE, I SAW D'ERLANGER. ♥ I WENT TO DESPAIRS RAY ♥ ON THE 30TH, AND I SAW BOOGIEMAN AT CC LEMON HALL ON THE 31ST, BUT THEY ONLY PLAYED ONE SONG. THEN I HEADED TO THE SHINJUKU LOFT FOR THE COUNTDOWN CONCERT WITH NEW ROTE'KA. ♥ I WENT CRAZY. ♥ AT 1 AM, THE SLUT BANKS CAME ONSTAGE FOR A REUNION SHOW. ♥ ♥ ♥ AS SOON AS I HEARD TUSK'S VOICE, I STARTED SWOONING. ♥ ON JANUARY 2ND, I SAW KIYOHARU-SAMA. ♥ SIGH...I WAS IN PARADISE. ♥ ♥ ♥

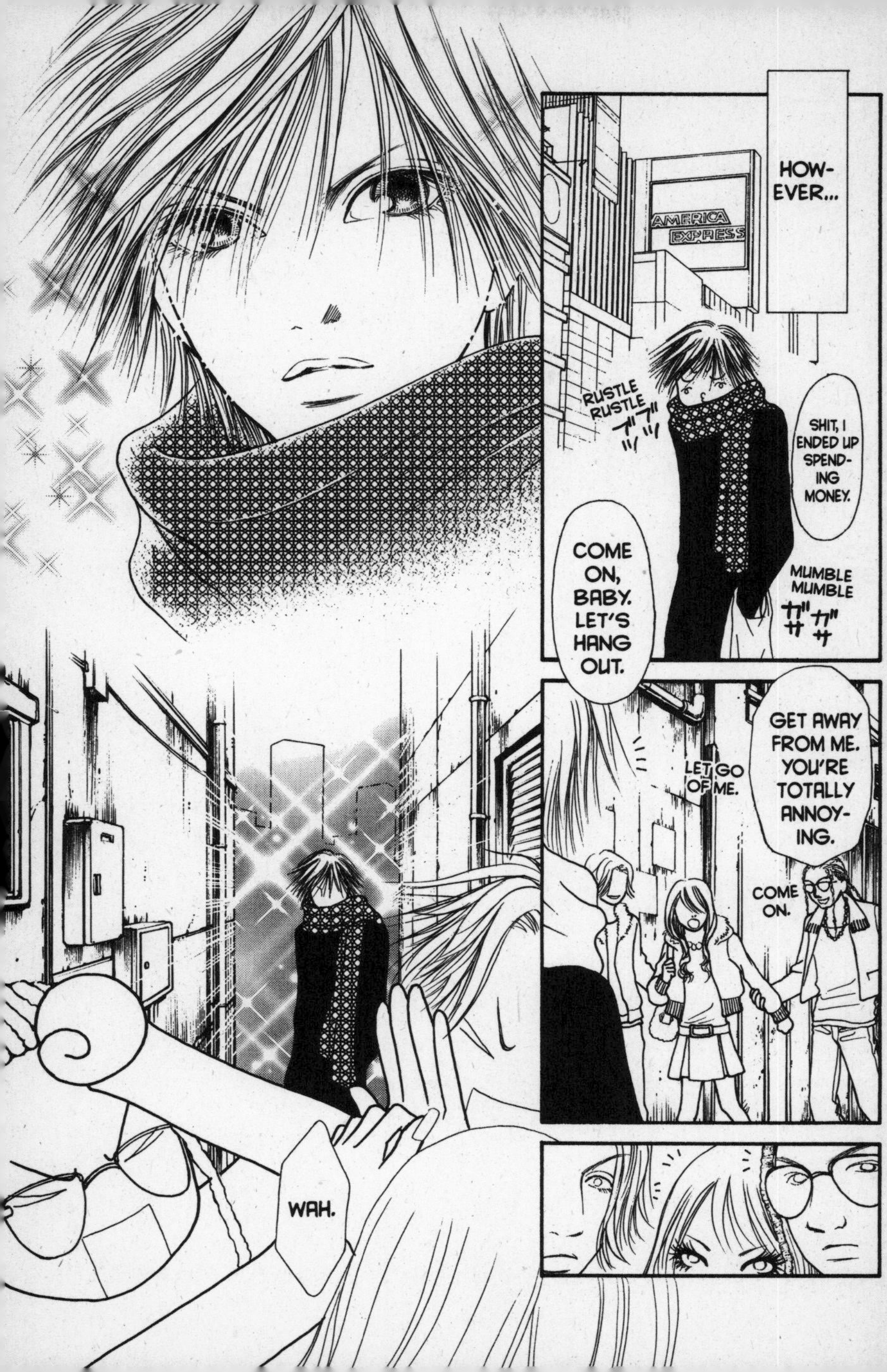
HOW-EVER...
AMERICA EXPRESS
RUSTLE RUSTLE
ブツブツ
SHIT, I ENDED UP SPEND-ING MONEY.
MUMBLE MUMBLE
ガサガサ
COME ON, BABY. LET'S HANG OUT.
GET AWAY FROM ME. YOU'RE TOTALLY ANNOY-ING.
LET GO OF ME.
COME ON.
WAH.

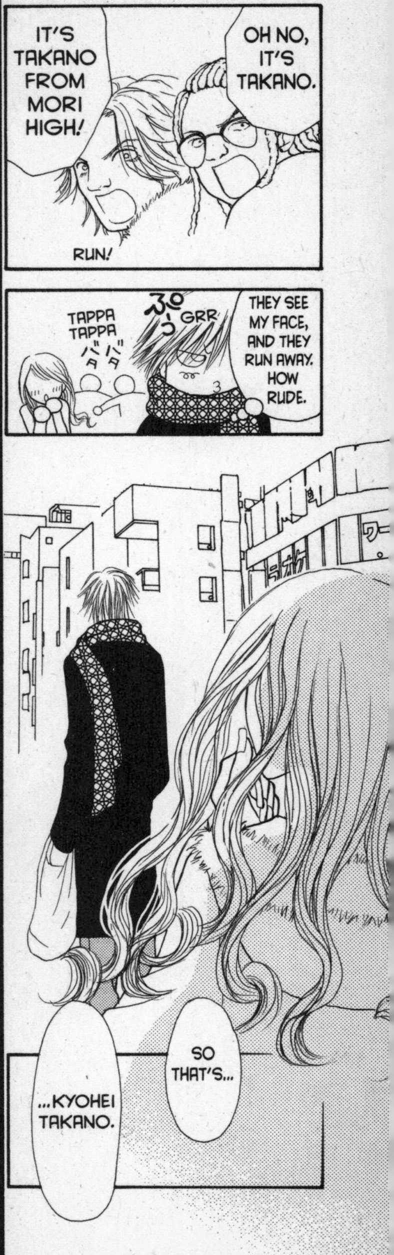
OH NO, IT'S TAKANO.
IT'S TAKANO FROM MORI HIGH!
RUN!
THEY SEE MY FACE, AND THEY RUN AWAY. HOW RUDE.
GRR
TAPPA TAPPA
SO THAT'S...
...KYOHEI TAKANO.

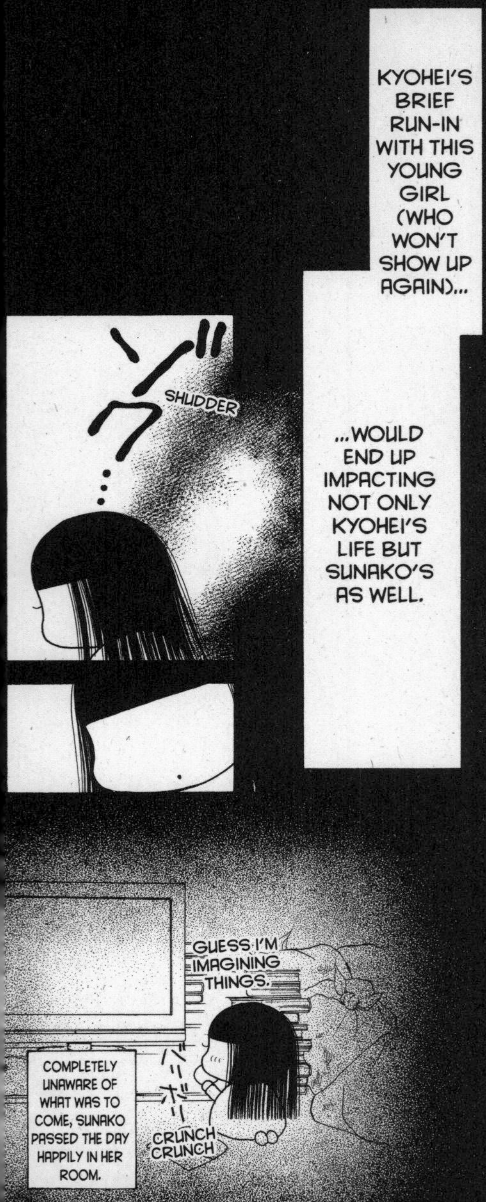
KYOHEI'S BRIEF RUN-IN WITH THIS YOUNG GIRL (WHO WON'T SHOW UP AGAIN)...
...WOULD END UP IMPACTING NOT ONLY KYOHEI'S LIFE BUT SUNAKO'S AS WELL.
ゾク...
SHUDDER
GUESS I'M IMAGINING THINGS.
バリボリ
CRUNCH CRUNCH
COMPLETELY UNAWARE OF WHAT WAS TO COME, SUNAKO PASSED THE DAY HAPPILY IN HER ROOM.

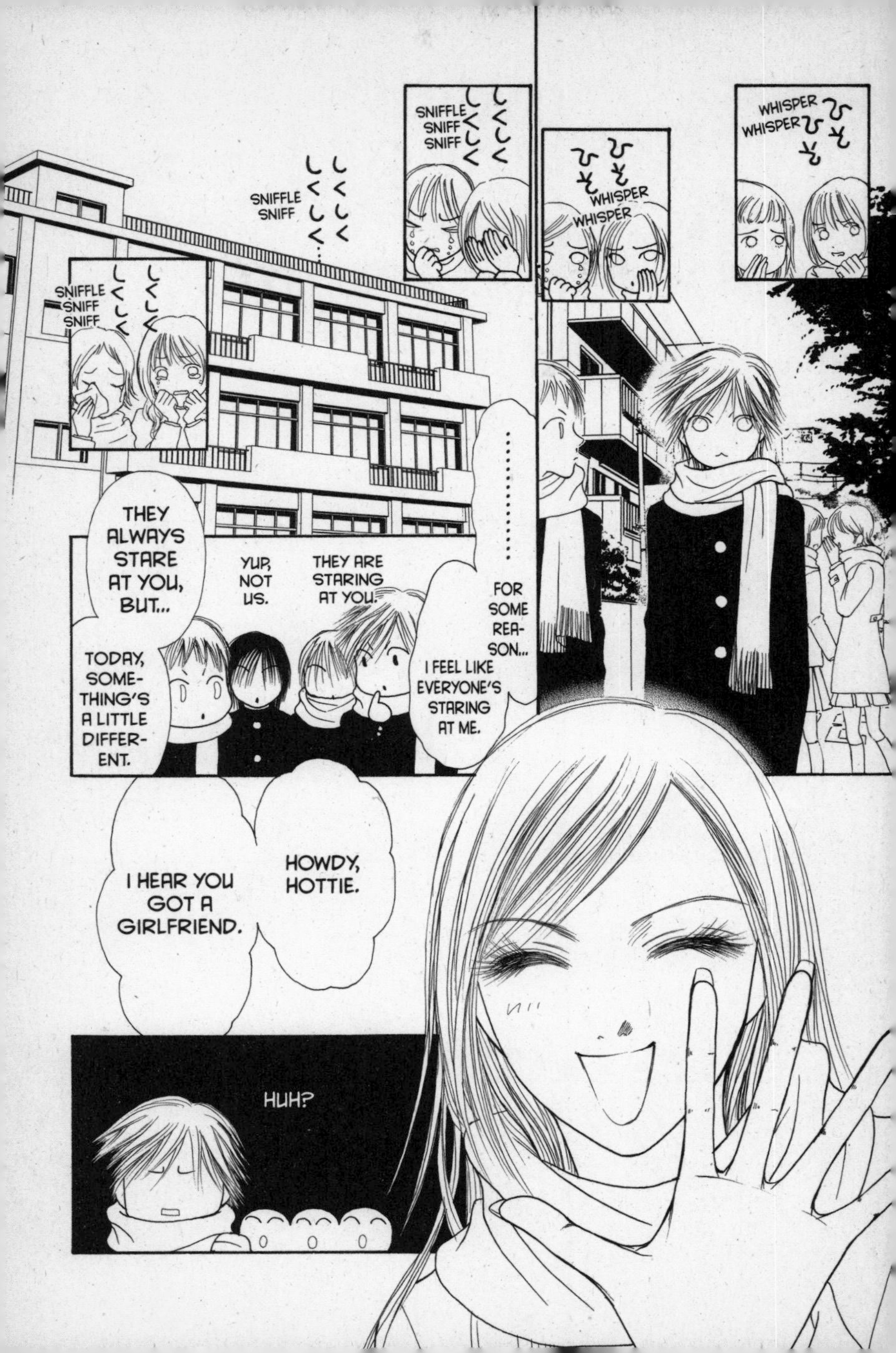

WHISPER WHISPER
ひそひそ
ひそひそ
WHISPER WHISPER
......
FOR SOME REA-SON...
I FEEL LIKE EVERYONE'S STARING AT ME.
しくしくしく
SNIFFLE SNIFF SNIFF
しくしく
SNIFFLE SNIFF
しくしくしく
SNIFFLE SNIFF SNIFF
THEY ARE STARING AT YOU.
YUP, NOT US.
THEY ALWAYS STARE AT YOU, BUT...
TODAY, SOME-THING'S A LITTLE DIFFER-ENT.
HOWDY, HOTTIE.
I HEAR YOU GOT A GIRLFRIEND.
HUH?

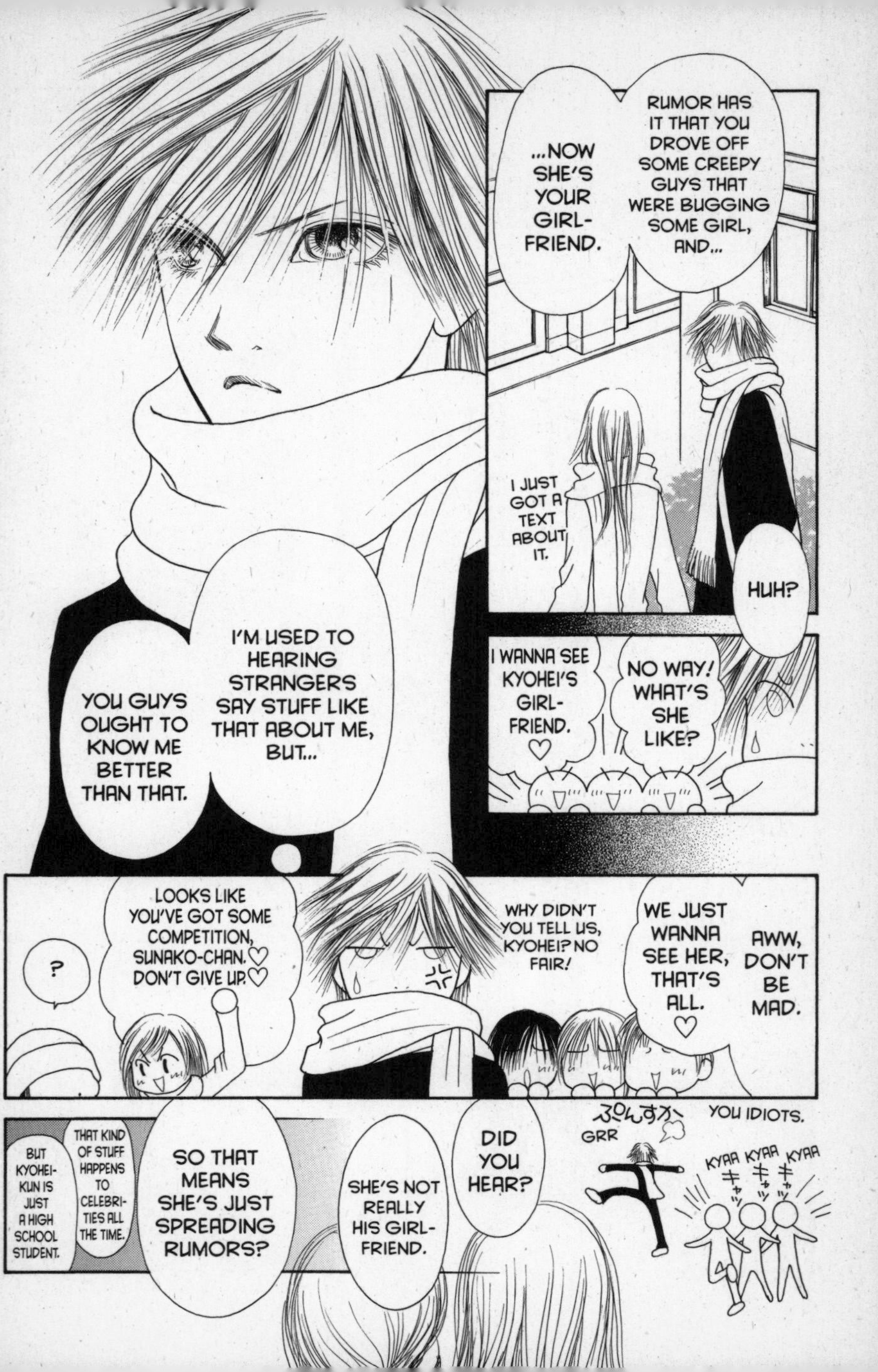
RUMOR HAS IT THAT YOU DROVE OFF SOME CREEPY GUYS THAT WERE BUGGING SOME GIRL, AND...
...NOW SHE'S YOUR GIRL-FRIEND.
I JUST GOT A TEXT ABOUT IT.
HUH?
NO WAY! WHAT'S SHE LIKE?
I WANNA SEE KYOHEI'S GIRL-FRIEND. ♡
I'M USED TO HEARING STRANGERS SAY STUFF LIKE THAT ABOUT ME, BUT...
YOU GUYS OUGHT TO KNOW ME BETTER THAN THAT.
AWW, DON'T BE MAD.
WE JUST WANNA SEE HER, THAT'S ALL. ♡
WHY DIDN'T YOU TELL US, KYOHEI? NO FAIR!
LOOKS LIKE YOU'VE GOT SOME COMPETITION, SUNAKO-CHAN.♡ DON'T GIVE UP.♡
?
YOU IDIOTS.
ぷんすか
GRR
KYAA KYAA KYAA
キャッ キャッ キャッ
DID YOU HEAR?
SHE'S NOT REALLY HIS GIRL-FRIEND.
SO THAT MEANS SHE'S JUST SPREADING RUMORS?
THAT KIND OF STUFF HAPPENS TO CELEBRITIES ALL THE TIME.
BUT KYOHEI-KUN IS JUST A HIGH SCHOOL STUDENT.

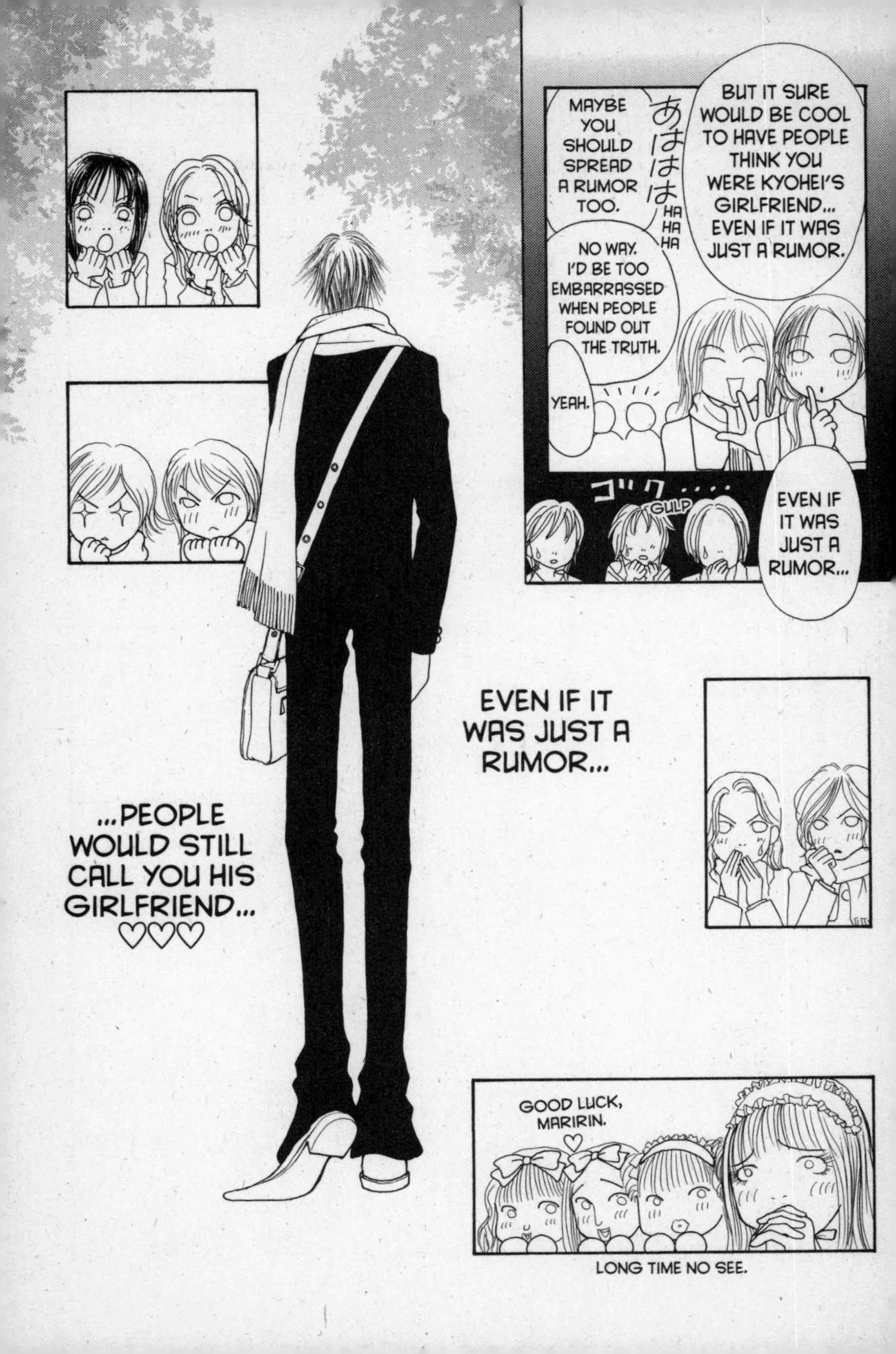

BUT IT SURE WOULD BE COOL TO HAVE PEOPLE THINK YOU WERE KYOHEI'S GIRLFRIEND... EVEN IF IT WAS JUST A RUMOR.
あははは
HA HA HA
MAYBE YOU SHOULD SPREAD A RUMOR TOO.
NO WAY. I'D BE TOO EMBARRASSED WHEN PEOPLE FOUND OUT THE TRUTH.
YEAH.
EVEN IF IT WAS JUST A RUMOR...
ゴック
GULP
EVEN IF IT WAS JUST A RUMOR...
...PEOPLE WOULD STILL CALL YOU HIS GIRLFRIEND... ♡♡♡
GOOD LUCK, MARIRIN. ♡
LONG TIME NO SEE.

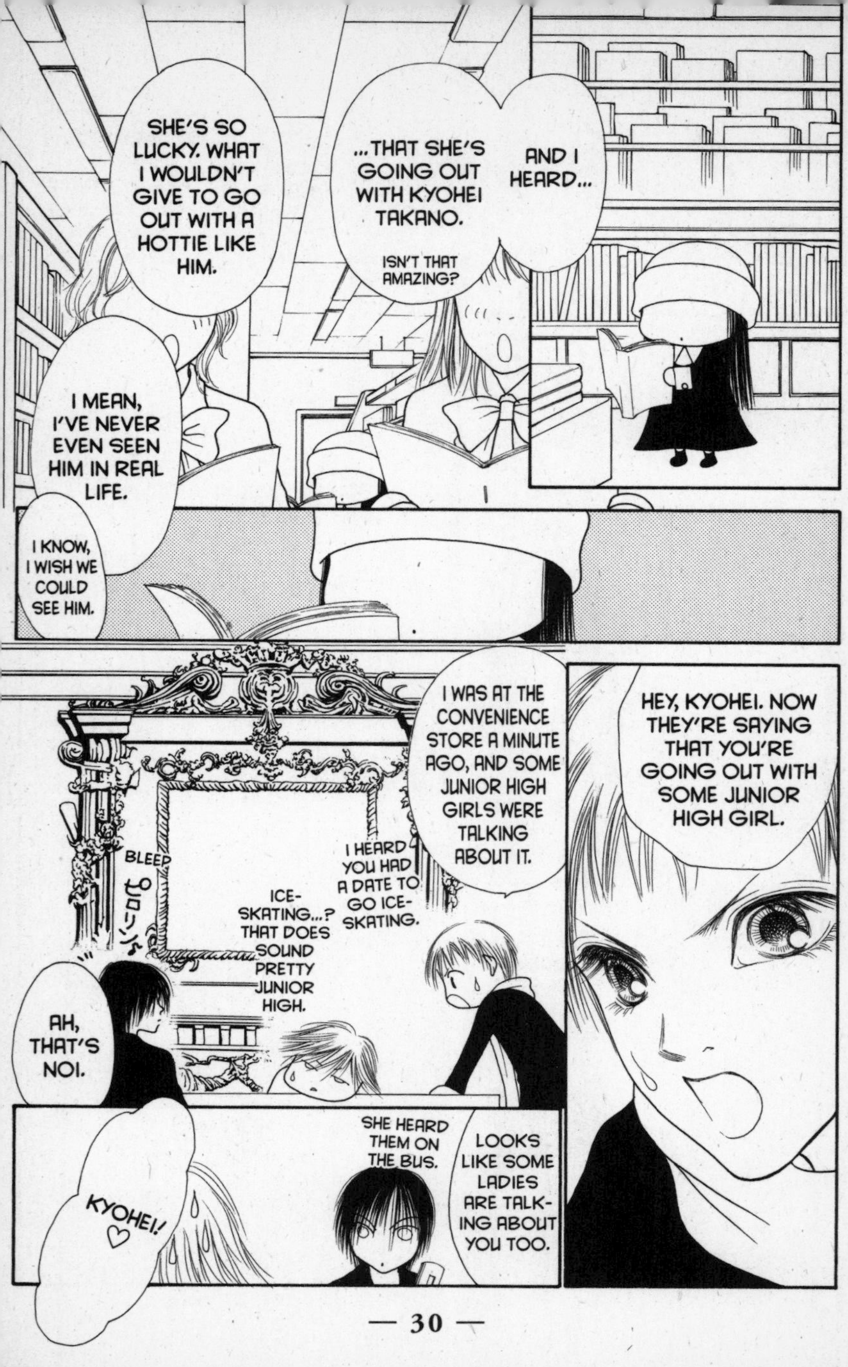

AND I HEARD...
...THAT SHE'S GOING OUT WITH KYOHEI TAKANO.
ISN'T THAT AMAZING?
SHE'S SO LUCKY. WHAT I WOULDN'T GIVE TO GO OUT WITH A HOTTIE LIKE HIM.
I MEAN, I'VE NEVER EVEN SEEN HIM IN REAL LIFE.
I KNOW, I WISH WE COULD SEE HIM.
HEY, KYOHEI. NOW THEY'RE SAYING THAT YOU'RE GOING OUT WITH SOME JUNIOR HIGH GIRL.
I WAS AT THE CONVENIENCE STORE A MINUTE AGO, AND SOME JUNIOR HIGH GIRLS WERE TALKING ABOUT IT.
I HEARD YOU HAD A DATE TO GO ICE-SKATING.
ICE-SKATING...? THAT DOES SOUND PRETTY JUNIOR HIGH.
BLEEP
ピロリン♪
AH, THAT'S NOI.
LOOKS LIKE SOME LADIES ARE TALKING ABOUT YOU TOO.
SHE HEARD THEM ON THE BUS.
KYOHEI! ♥

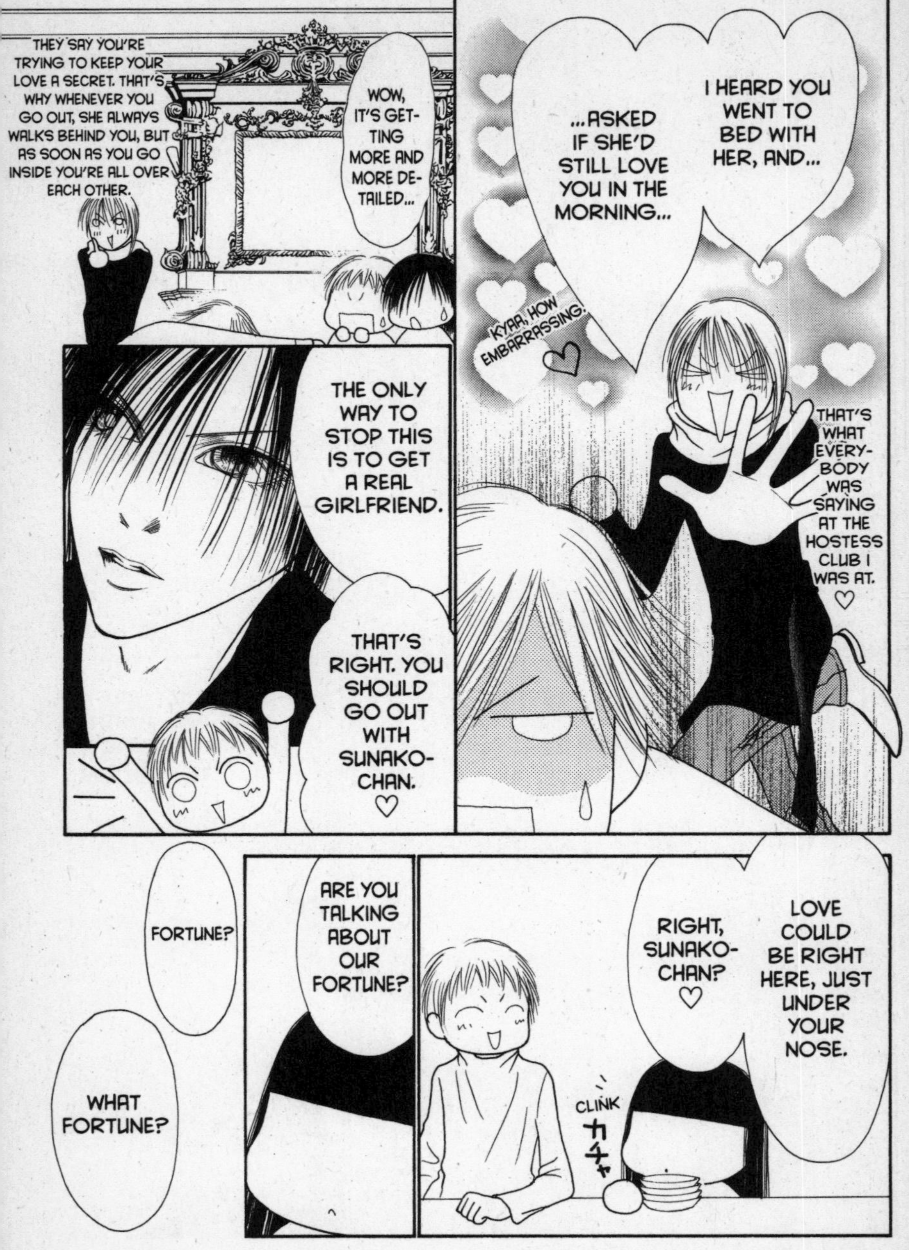
I HEARD YOU WENT TO BED WITH HER, AND...
...ASKED IF SHE'D STILL LOVE YOU IN THE MORNING...
KYAA, HOW EMBARRASSING! ♡
THAT'S WHAT EVERYBODY WAS SAYING AT THE HOSTESS CLUB I WAS AT. ♡
WOW, IT'S GETTING MORE AND MORE DETAILED...
THEY SAY YOU'RE TRYING TO KEEP YOUR LOVE A SECRET. THAT'S WHY WHENEVER YOU GO OUT, SHE ALWAYS WALKS BEHIND YOU, BUT AS SOON AS YOU GO INSIDE YOU'RE ALL OVER EACH OTHER.
THE ONLY WAY TO STOP THIS IS TO GET A REAL GIRLFRIEND.
THAT'S RIGHT. YOU SHOULD GO OUT WITH SUNAKO-CHAN. ♡
LOVE COULD BE RIGHT HERE, JUST UNDER YOUR NOSE.
RIGHT, SUNAKO-CHAN? ♡
CLINK
カチャ
ARE YOU TALKING ABOUT OUR FORTUNE?
FORTUNE?
WHAT FORTUNE?

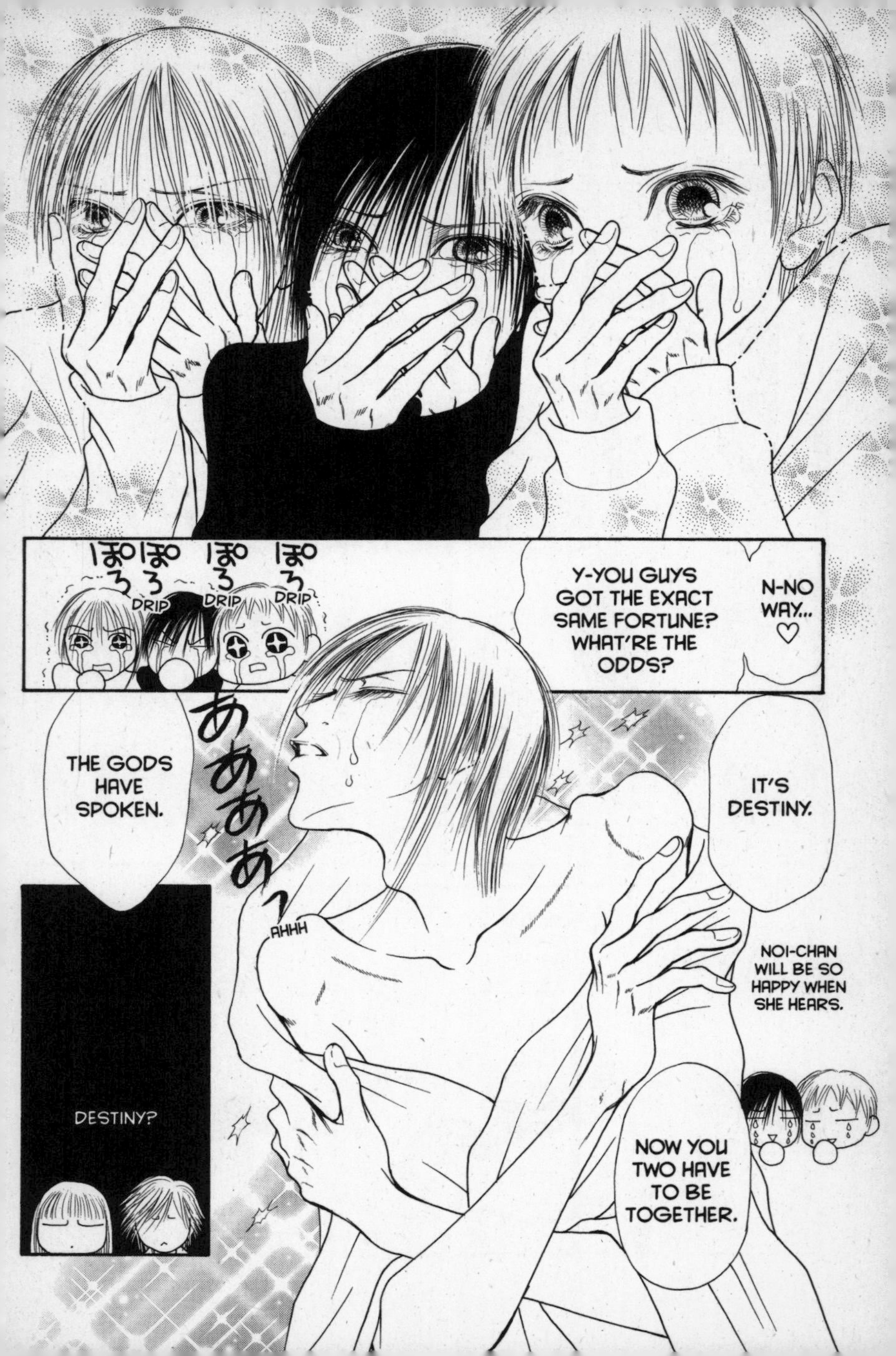
N-NO WAY... ♡
Y-YOU GUYS GOT THE EXACT SAME FORTUNE? WHAT'RE THE ODDS?
ぽろぽろ DRIP
ぽろ DRIP
ぽろ DRIP
IT'S DESTINY.
THE GODS HAVE SPOKEN.
ああああ AHHH
NOI-CHAN WILL BE SO HAPPY WHEN SHE HEARS.
NOW YOU TWO HAVE TO BE TOGETHER.
DESTINY?

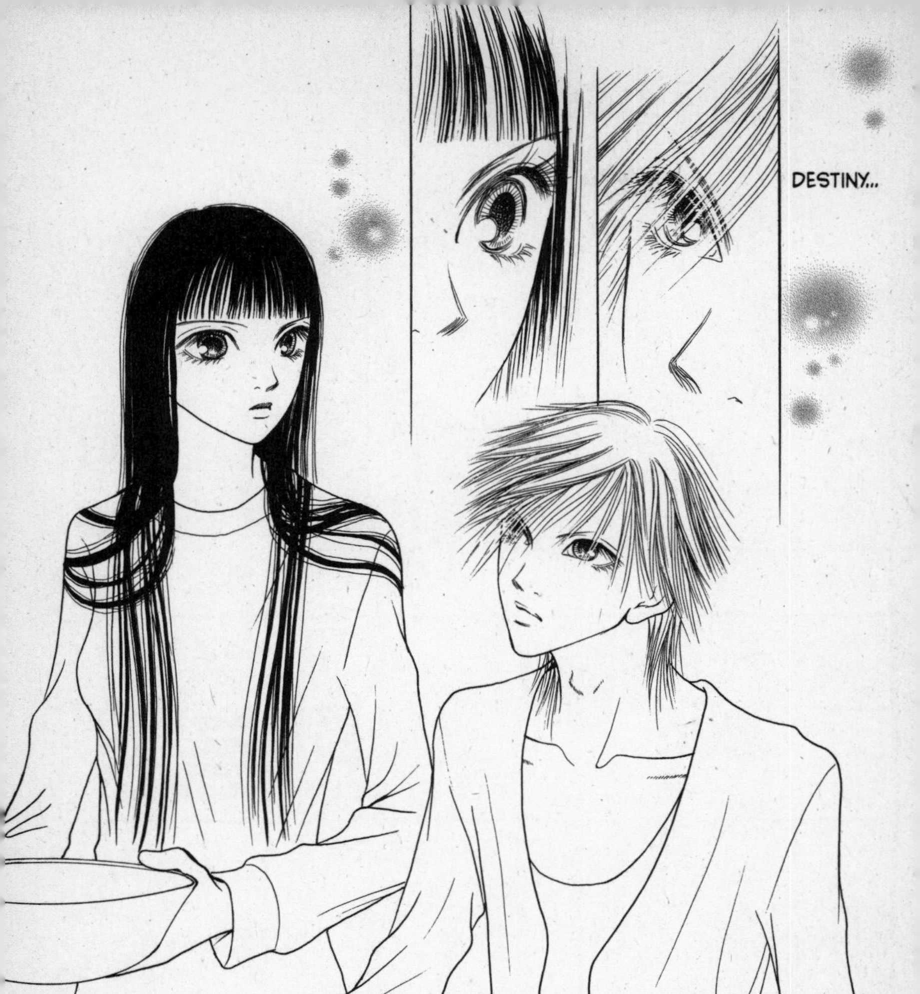
DESTINY...
WHAT? NOT STIR-FRIED VEGGIES AGAIN!
HOW ABOUT A NICE THICK, JUICY STEAK ONCE IN A WHILE?
WE DON'T HAVE THAT KIND OF MONEY.
IF YOU HAVE MONEY FOR CARROTS, YOU HAVE MONEY FOR MEAT.
SHUT UP, GO BUY SOME YOUR-SELF THEN.
KYOHEI!

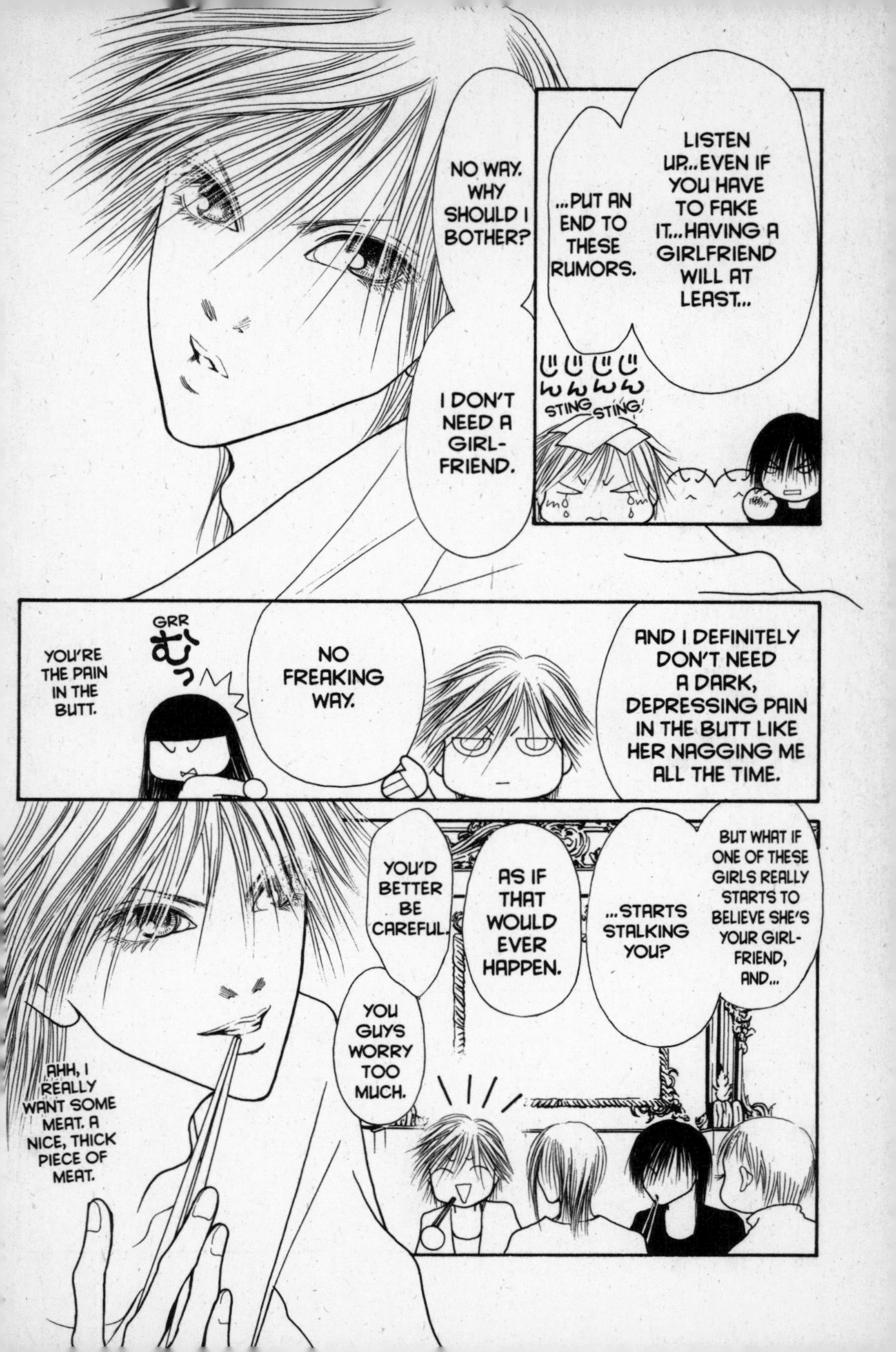
LISTEN UP...EVEN IF YOU HAVE TO FAKE IT...HAVING A GIRLFRIEND WILL AT LEAST...
...PUT AN END TO THESE RUMORS.
じんじんじんじん
STING STING
NO WAY. WHY SHOULD I BOTHER?
I DON'T NEED A GIRL-FRIEND.
AND I DEFINITELY DON'T NEED A DARK, DEPRESSING PAIN IN THE BUTT LIKE HER NAGGING ME ALL THE TIME.
NO FREAKING WAY.
むっ
GRR
YOU'RE THE PAIN IN THE BUTT.
BUT WHAT IF ONE OF THESE GIRLS REALLY STARTS TO BELIEVE SHE'S YOUR GIRL-FRIEND, AND...
...STARTS STALKING YOU?
AS IF THAT WOULD EVER HAPPEN.
YOU'D BETTER BE CAREFUL.
YOU GUYS WORRY TOO MUCH.
AHH, I REALLY WANT SOME MEAT. A NICE, THICK PIECE OF MEAT.

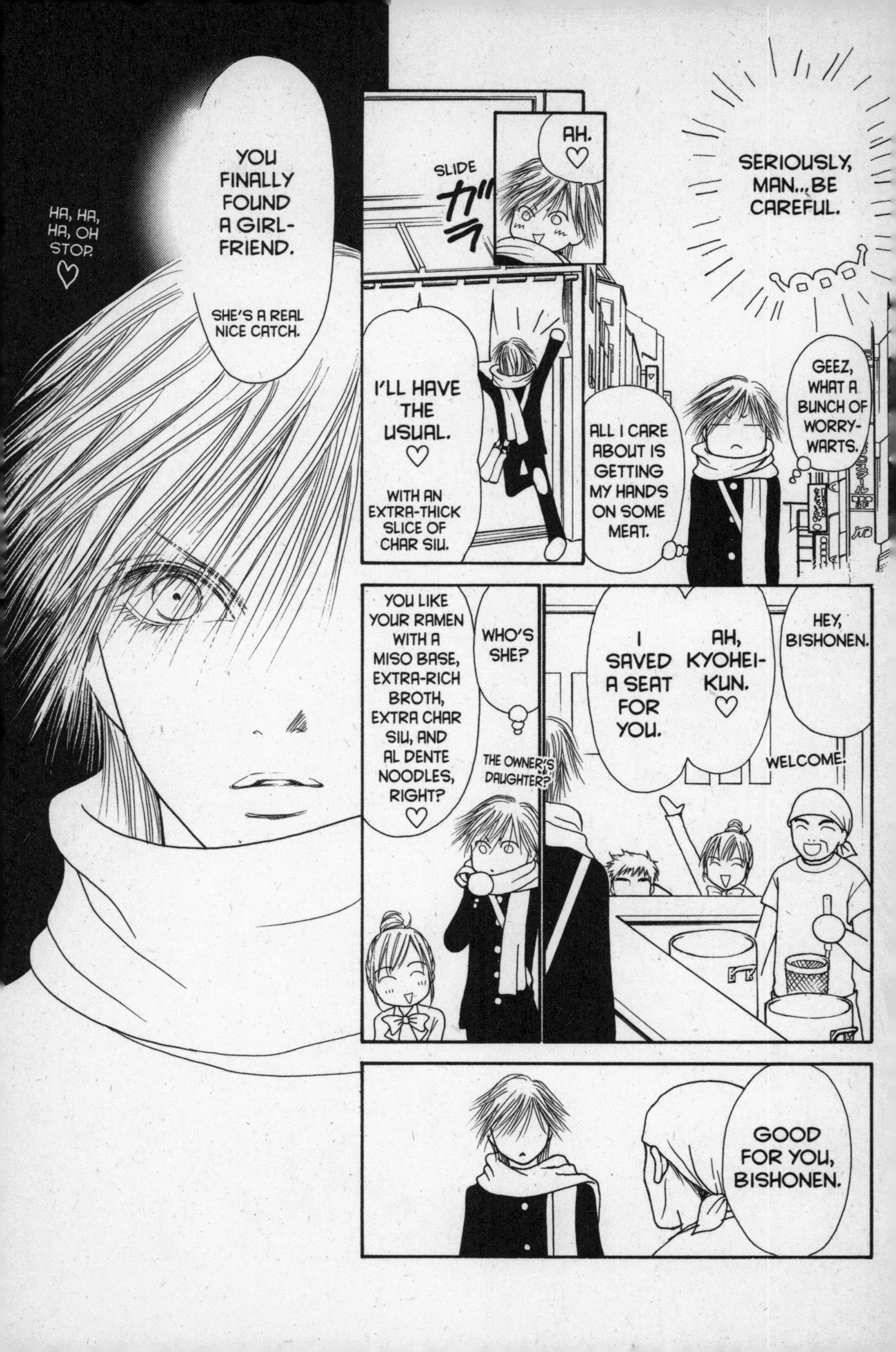
SERIOUSLY, MAN...BE CAREFUL.
AH. ♡
SLIDE
GEEZ, WHAT A BUNCH OF WORRY-WARTS.
ALL I CARE ABOUT IS GETTING MY HANDS ON SOME MEAT.
I'LL HAVE THE USUAL. ♡
WITH AN EXTRA-THICK SLICE OF CHAR SIU.
HEY, BISHONEN.
WELCOME.
AH, KYOHEI-KUN. ♡
I SAVED A SEAT FOR YOU.
WHO'S SHE?
THE OWNER'S DAUGHTER?
YOU LIKE YOUR RAMEN WITH A MISO BASE, EXTRA-RICH BROTH, EXTRA CHAR SIU, AND AL DENTE NOODLES, RIGHT? ♡
GOOD FOR YOU, BISHONEN.
YOU FINALLY FOUND A GIRL-FRIEND.
SHE'S A REAL NICE CATCH.
HA, HA, HA, OH STOP. ♡

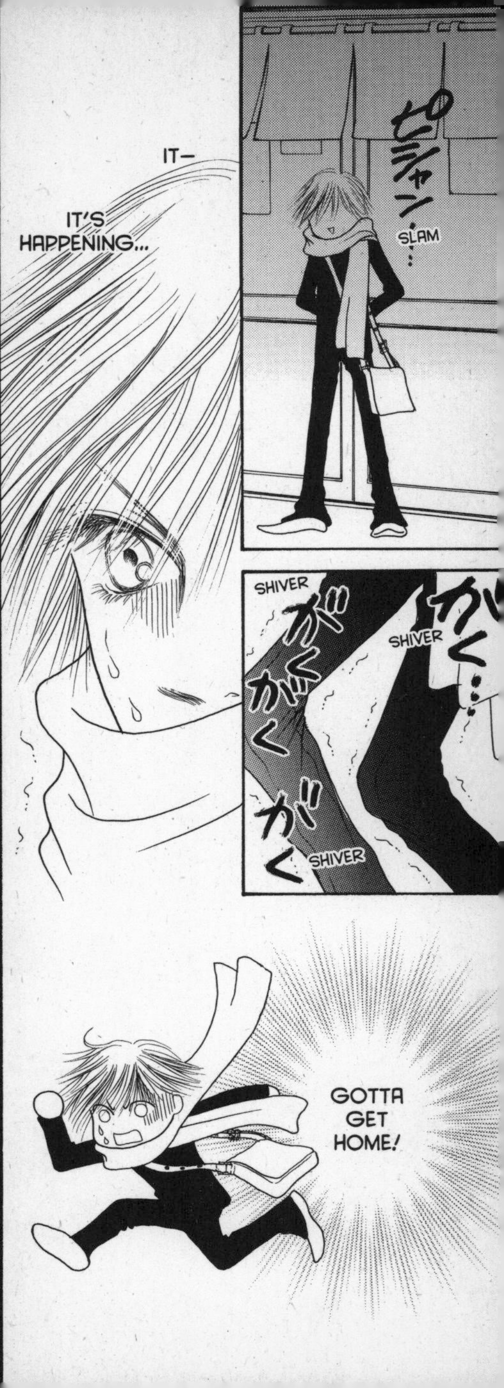
ピシャン
SLAM
SHIVER
がくがくがく
SHIVER
がく
SHIVER
がく…
IT—
IT'S HAPPENING...
GOTTA GET HOME!
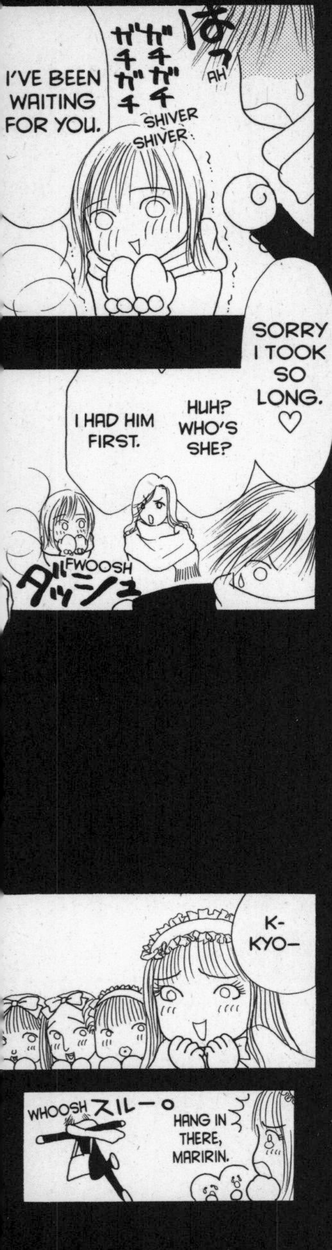
はっ
AH
ガチガチガチガチ
SHIVER SHIVER
I'VE BEEN WAITING FOR YOU.
SORRY I TOOK SO LONG. ♡
HUH? WHO'S SHE?
I HAD HIM FIRST.
FWOOSH
ダッシュ
K-KYO—
HANG IN THERE, MARIRIN.
WHOOSH
スルー。

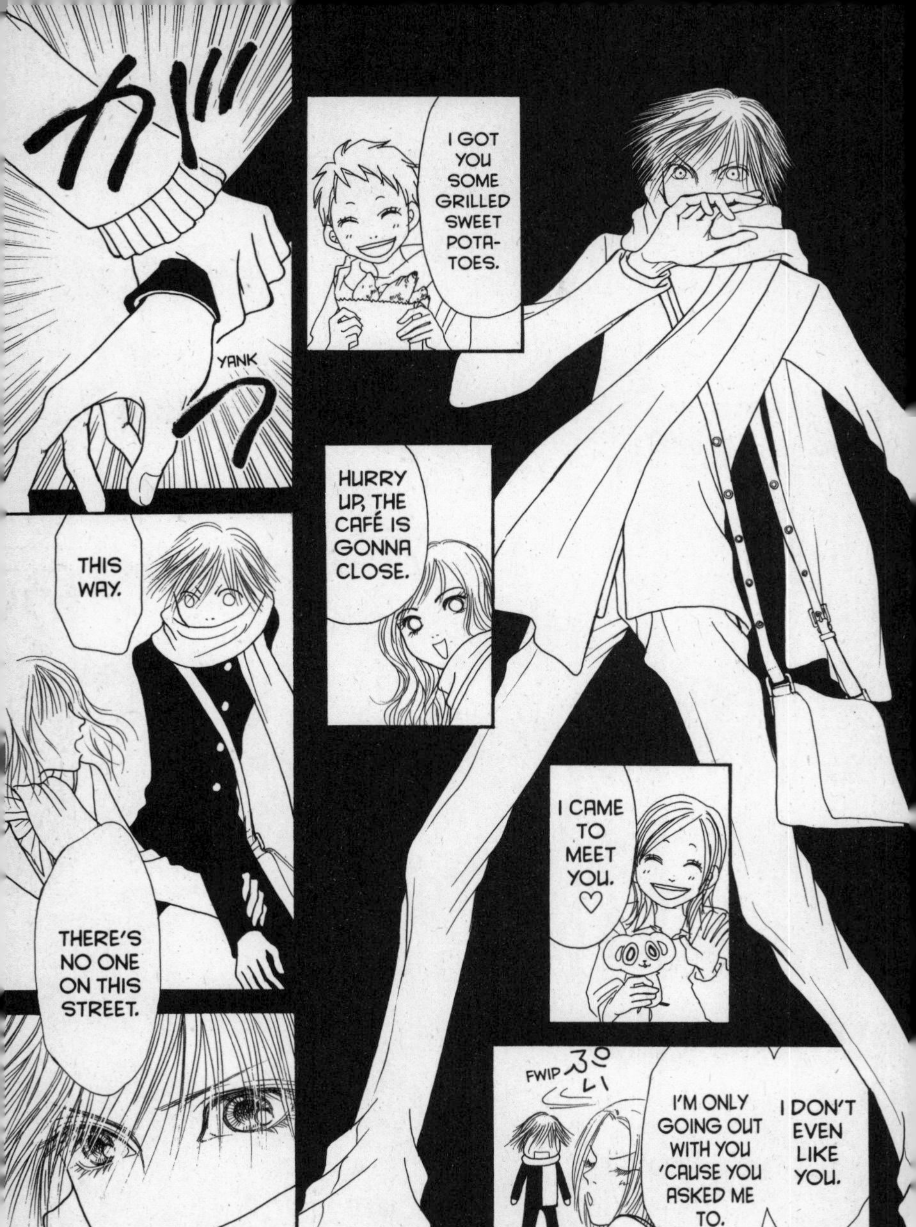
I GOT YOU SOME GRILLED SWEET POTA-TOES.
HURRY UP, THE CAFÉ IS GONNA CLOSE.
I CAME TO MEET YOU. ♡
FWIP
I DON'T EVEN LIKE YOU.
I'M ONLY GOING OUT WITH YOU 'CAUSE YOU ASKED ME TO.
THE EVER-SO-POPULAR TSUNDERE CHARACTER.
YANK
THIS WAY.
THERE'S NO ONE ON THIS STREET.

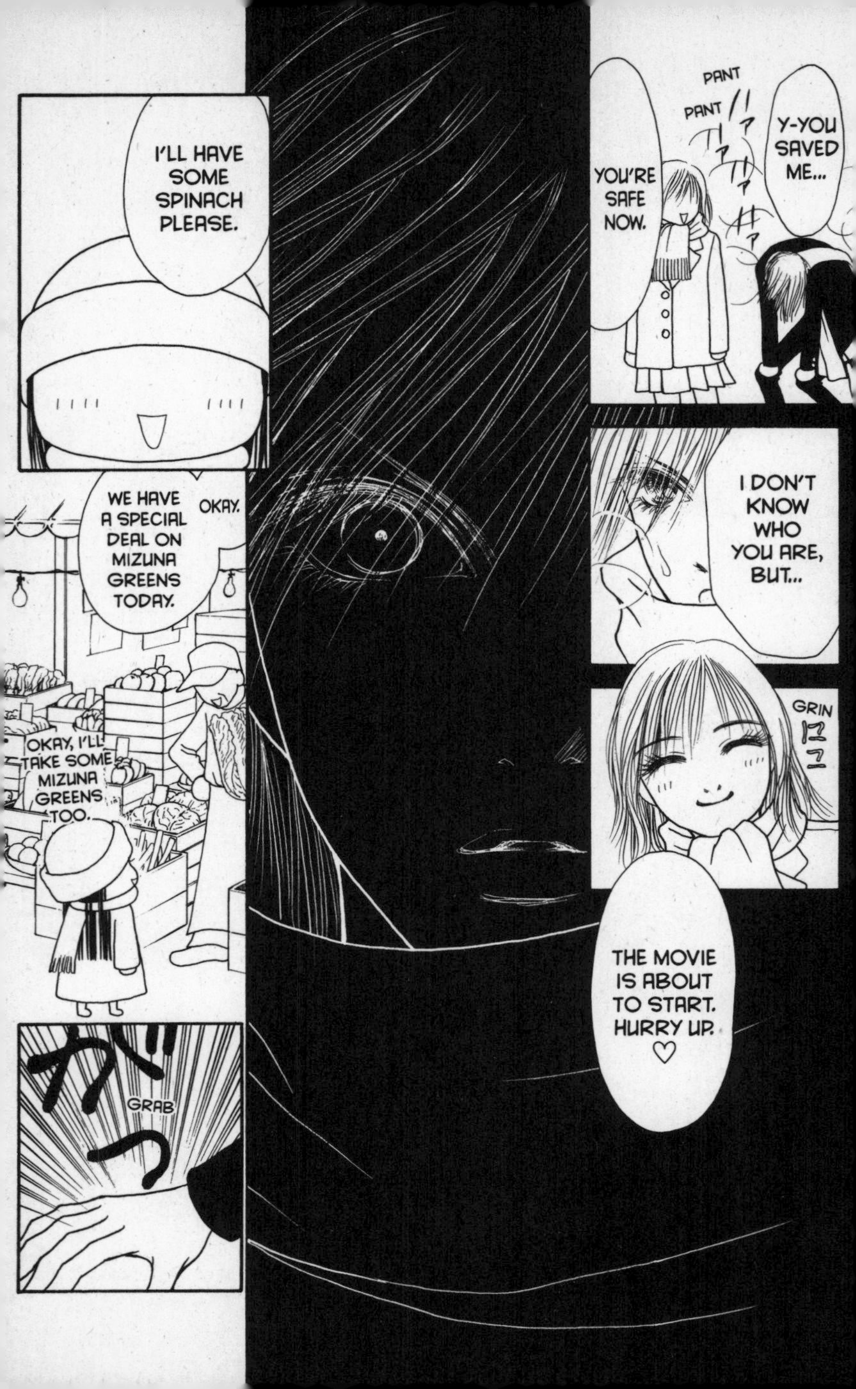
Y-YOU SAVED ME...
PANT
PANT
YOU'RE SAFE NOW.
I DON'T KNOW WHO YOU ARE, BUT...
GRIN
THE MOVIE IS ABOUT TO START. HURRY UP. ♡
I'LL HAVE SOME SPINACH PLEASE.
OKAY.
WE HAVE A SPECIAL DEAL ON MIZUNA GREENS TODAY.
OKAY, I'LL TAKE SOME MIZUNA GREENS TOO.
GRAB

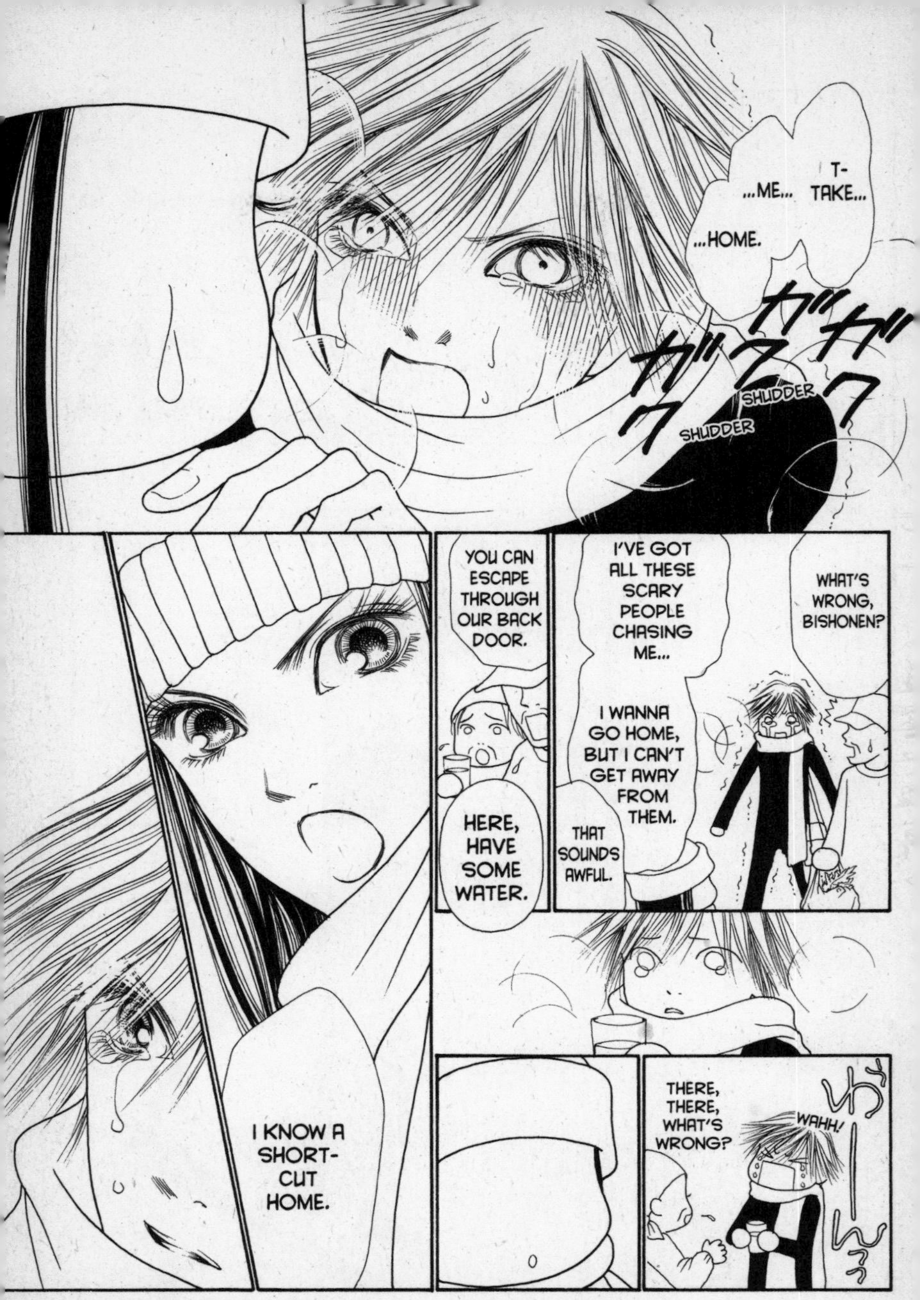
T- TAKE...
...ME...
...HOME.
SHUDDER
SHUDDER
WHAT'S WRONG, BISHONEN?
I'VE GOT ALL THESE SCARY PEOPLE CHASING ME...
I WANNA GO HOME, BUT I CAN'T GET AWAY FROM THEM.
THAT SOUNDS AWFUL.
YOU CAN ESCAPE THROUGH OUR BACK DOOR.
HERE, HAVE SOME WATER.
WAHH!
THERE, THERE, WHAT'S WRONG?
I KNOW A SHORT-CUT HOME.

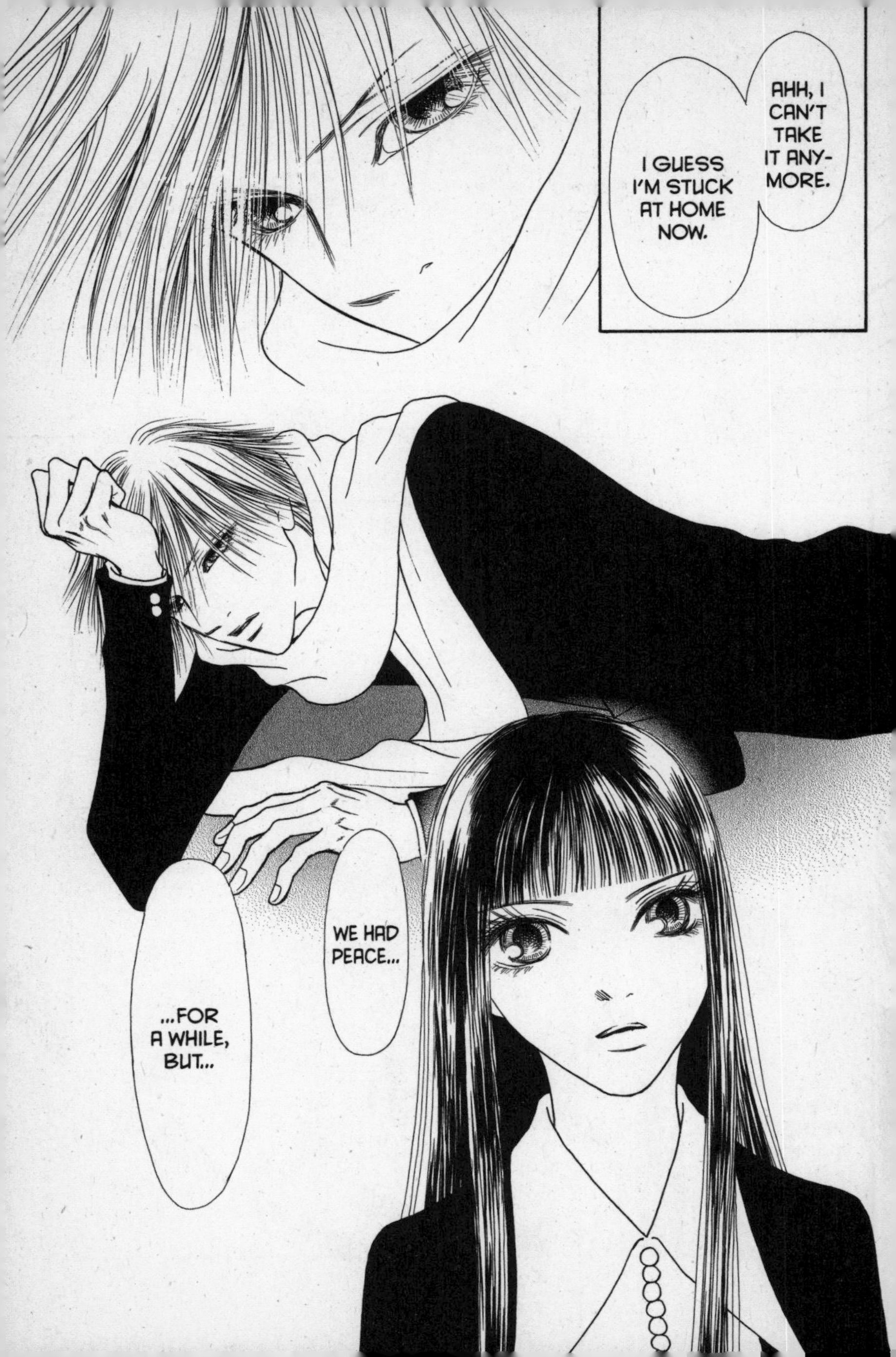
AHH, I CAN'T TAKE IT ANY-MORE.
I GUESS I'M STUCK AT HOME NOW.
WE HAD PEACE...
...FOR A WHILE, BUT...

— 42 —

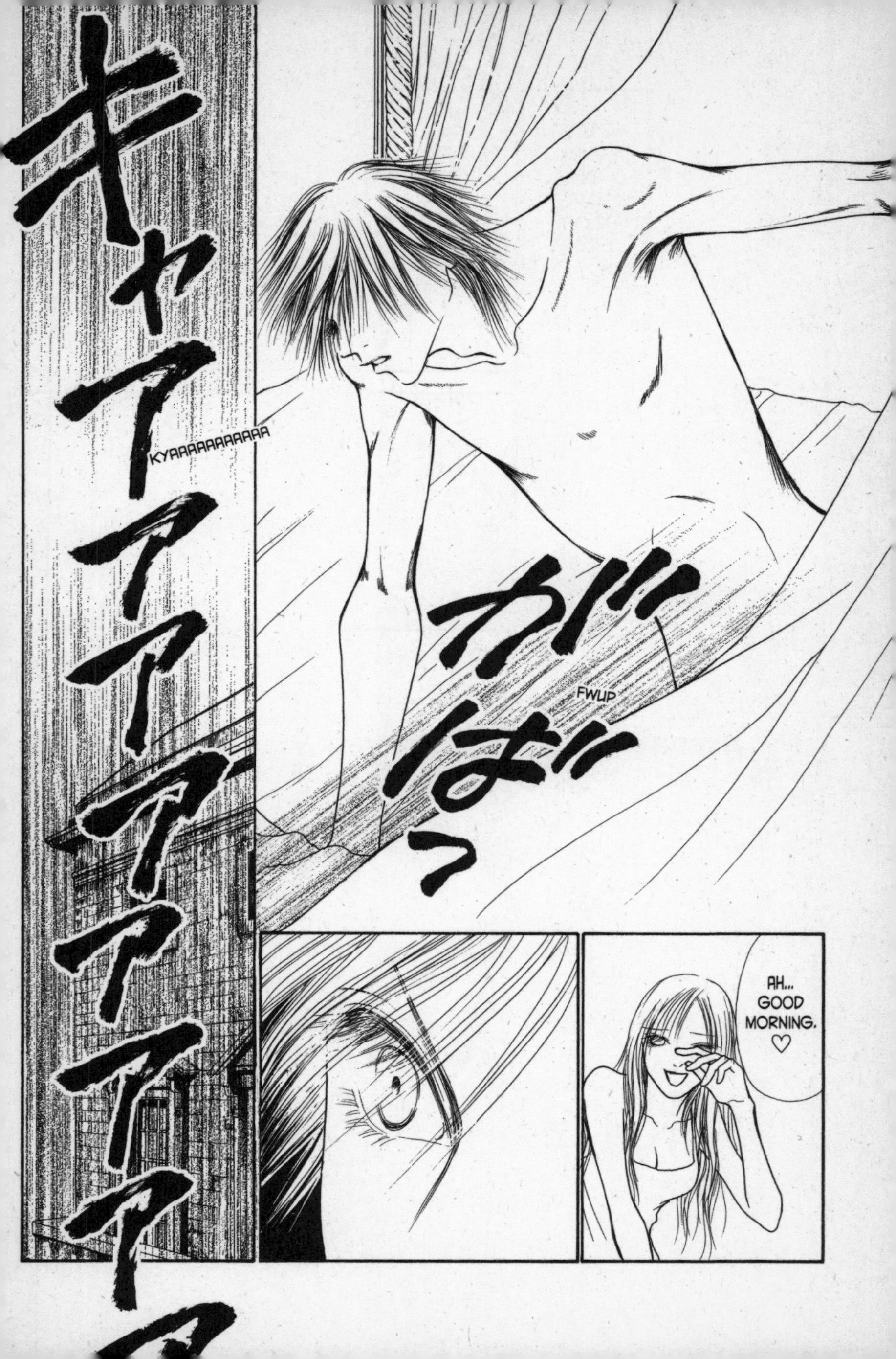
がばっ
FWUP
AH... GOOD MORNING. ♡
キャアアアアアアア
KYAAAAAAAAAAAA

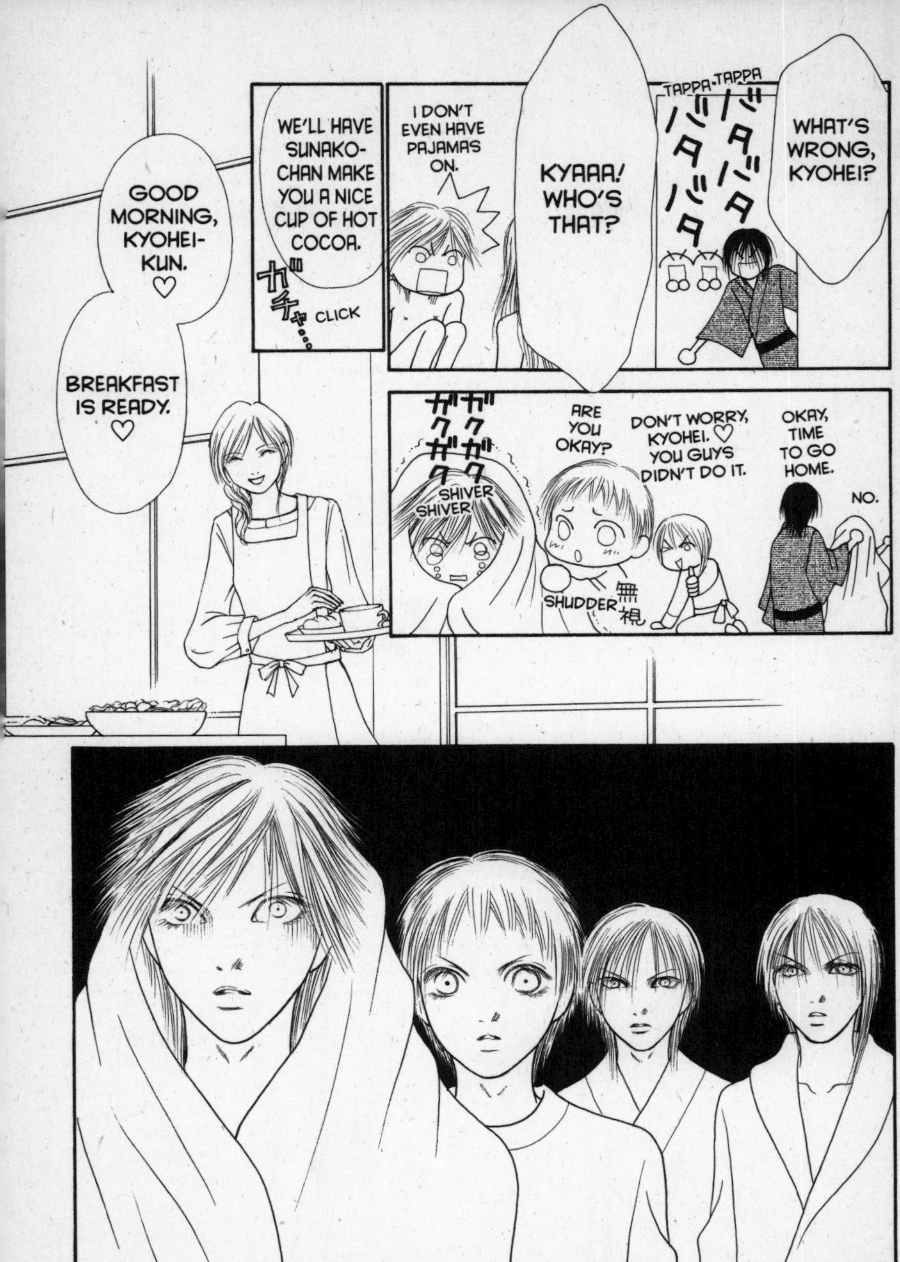
TAPPA-TAPPA
バタバタバタバタ
WHAT'S WRONG, KYOHEI?
KYAAA! WHO'S THAT?
I DON'T EVEN HAVE PAJAMAS ON.
WE'LL HAVE SUNAKO-CHAN MAKE YOU A NICE CUP OF HOT COCOA.
ガチャ…
CLICK
OKAY, TIME TO GO HOME.
NO.
DON'T WORRY, KYOHEI. ♡ YOU GUYS DIDN'T DO IT.
無視
ARE YOU OKAY?
SHUDDER
ガクガクガクガク
SHIVER SHIVER
GOOD MORNING, KYOHEI-KUN. ♡
BREAKFAST IS READY. ♡

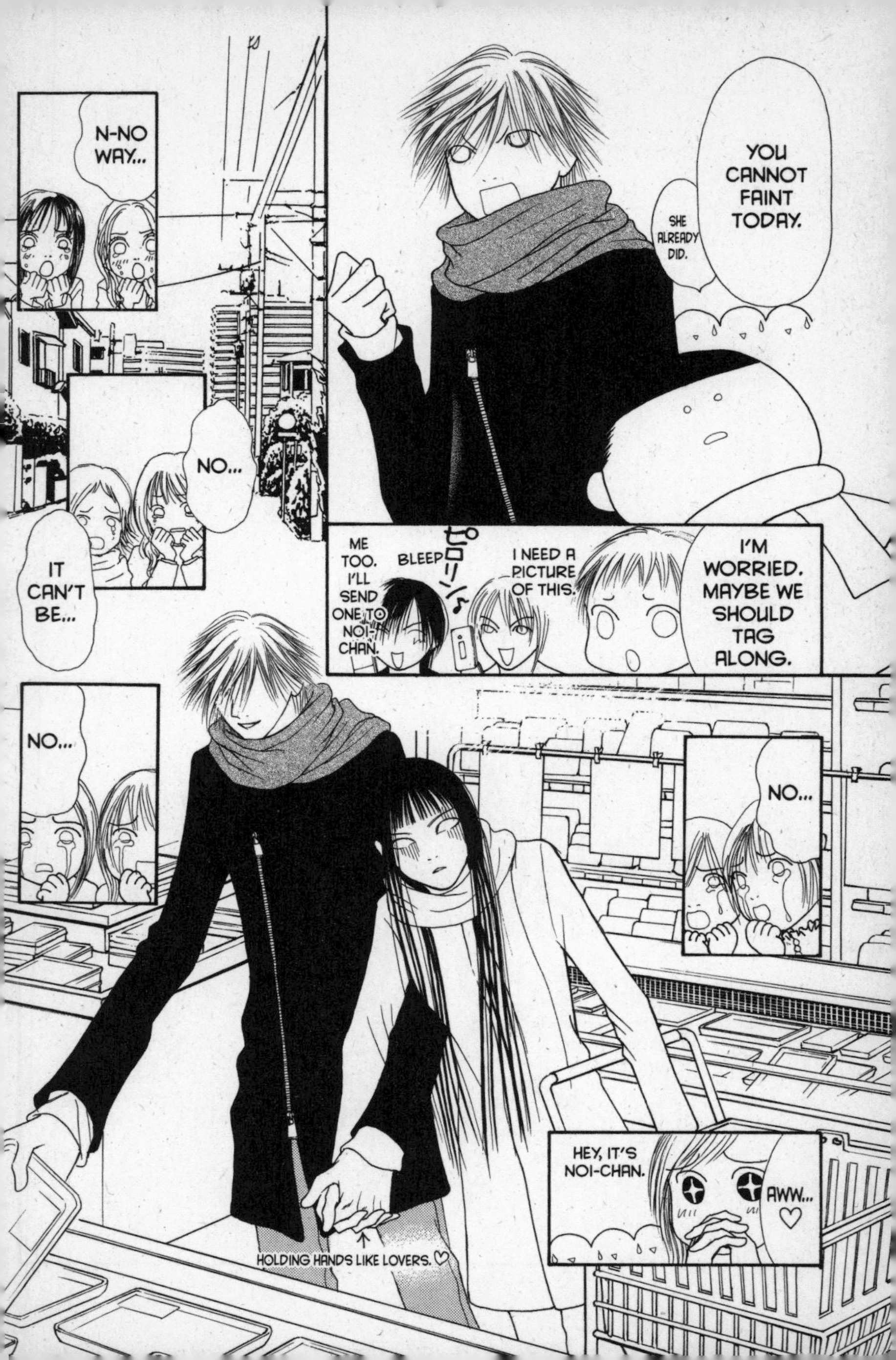
YOU CANNOT FAINT TODAY.
SHE ALREADY DID.
N-NO WAY...
NO...
IT CAN'T BE...
I'M WORRIED. MAYBE WE SHOULD TAG ALONG.
I NEED A PICTURE OF THIS.
ピロリ♪
BLEEP
ME TOO. I'LL SEND ONE TO NOI-CHAN.
NO...
AWW... ♡
HEY, IT'S NOI-CHAN.
HOLDING HANDS LIKE LOVERS. ♡
NO...

THAT'S HOW IN LOVE THEY LOOK...!!

NOOOOOO!!

AH

WE WENT SHOPPING, AND NOW WE'RE GOING HOME.

WH-WHERE ARE WE?

— 49 —

BESIDES, THOSE GIRLS ARE ALL GONE, SO I WANNA CELEBRATE.

D-DON'T TELL ME YOU BOUGHT A *BIG, THICK* STEAK.

AH.

I KNEW IT.

AT LEAST YOU BOUGHT ONE FOR EVERYONE.

Special Price 3980 Yen*

*$40

THEY WEREN'T AS THICK AS I WANTED, BUT...

SHUDDER SHUDDER

I'D HAVE DONE THIS EARLIER IF I'D KNOWN IT WOULD BE SO EASY.

I'M SURE WE'LL MANAGE.

NOW HOW ARE WE GONNA SURVIVE?

ALL GONE?

ALL GONE?

RUSTLE RUSTLE

YOU CHEATED ON ME!

WHO'S SHE?

SHIVER

KYOHEI-KUN...

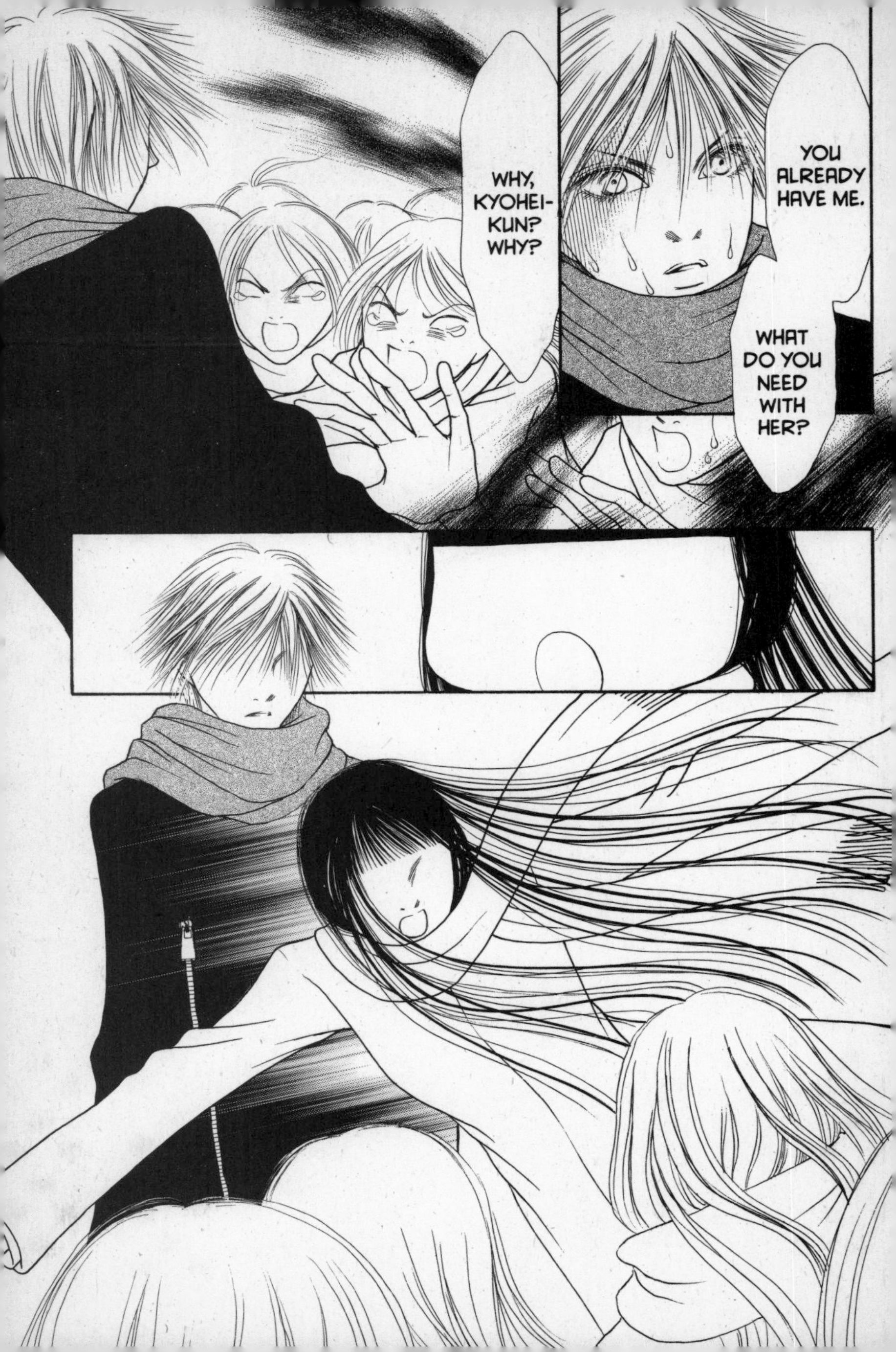
YOU ALREADY HAVE ME.
WHAT DO YOU NEED WITH HER?
WHY, KYOHEI-KUN? WHY?

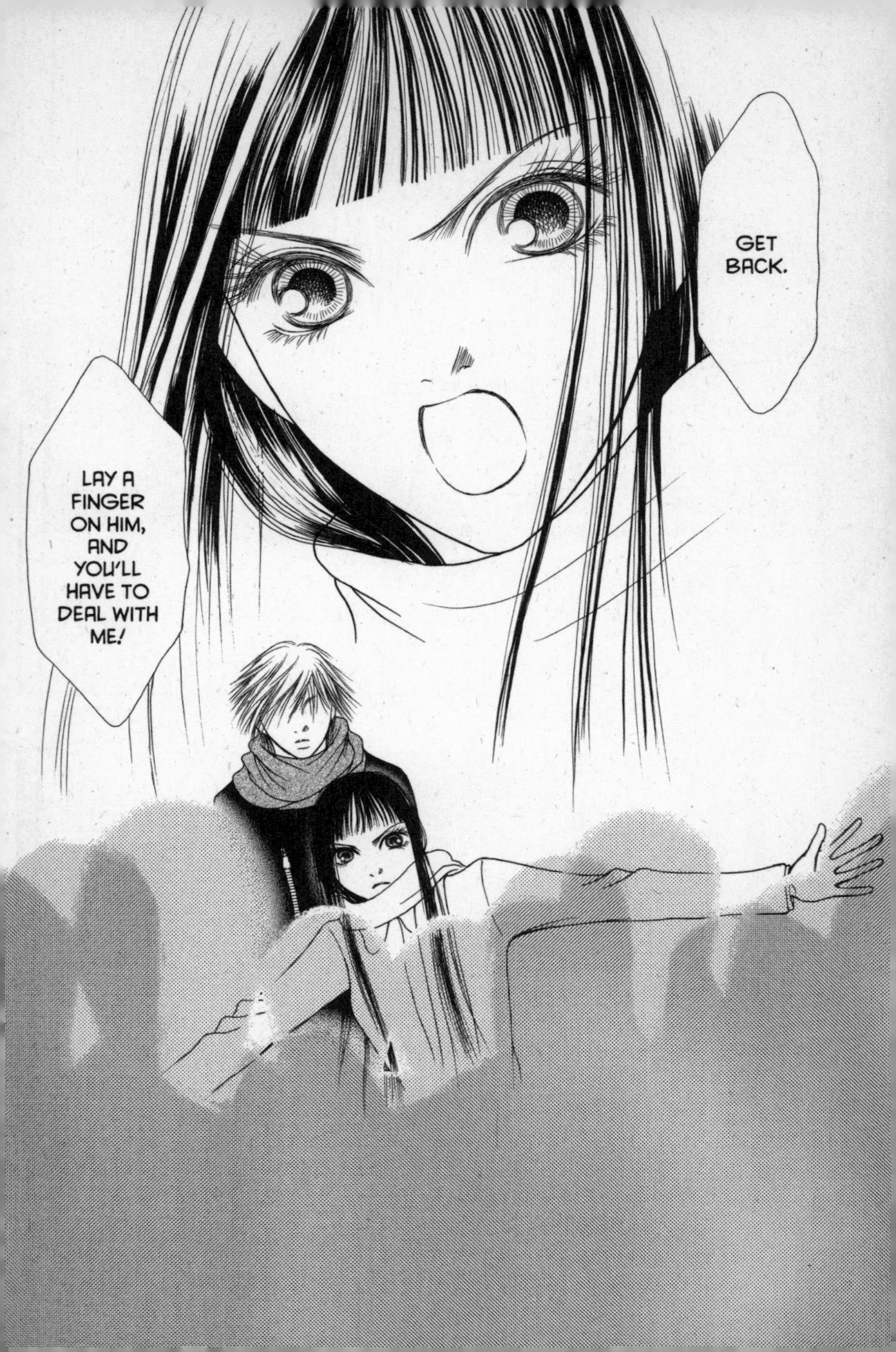
GET BACK.
LAY A FINGER ON HIM, AND YOU'LL HAVE TO DEAL WITH ME!

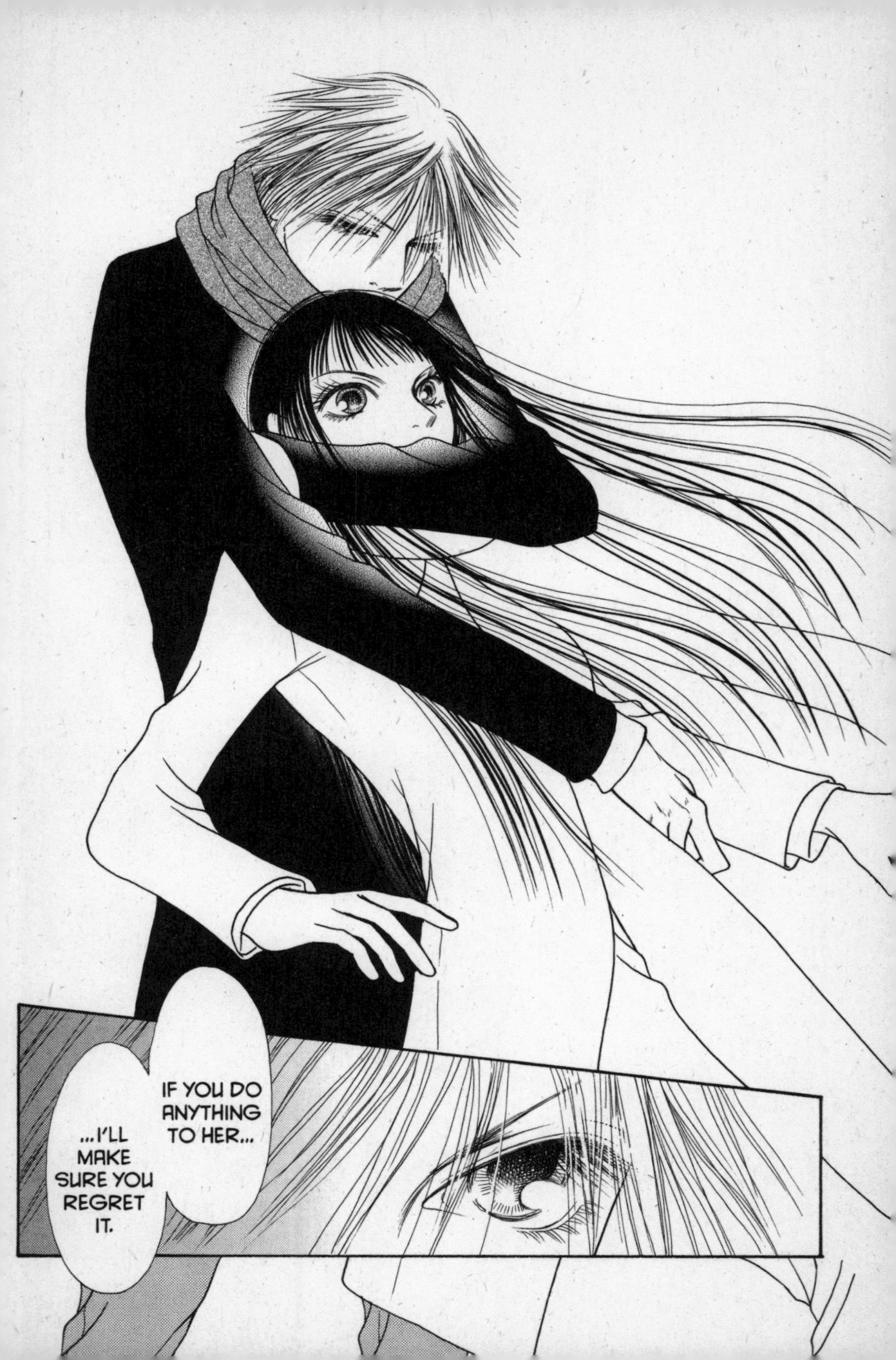
IF YOU DO ANYTHING TO HER...
...I'LL MAKE SURE YOU REGRET IT.

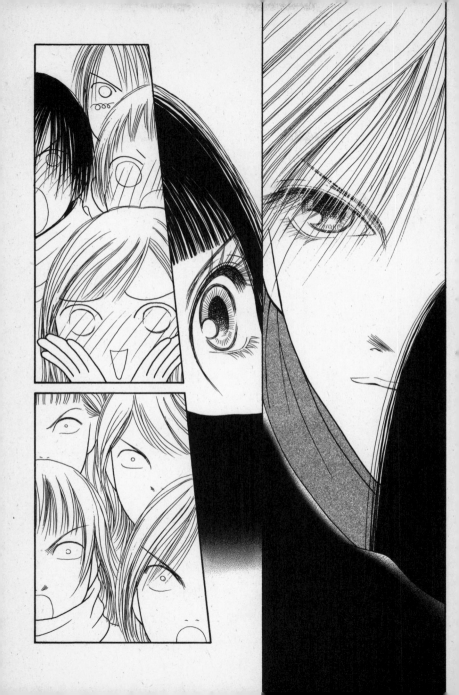

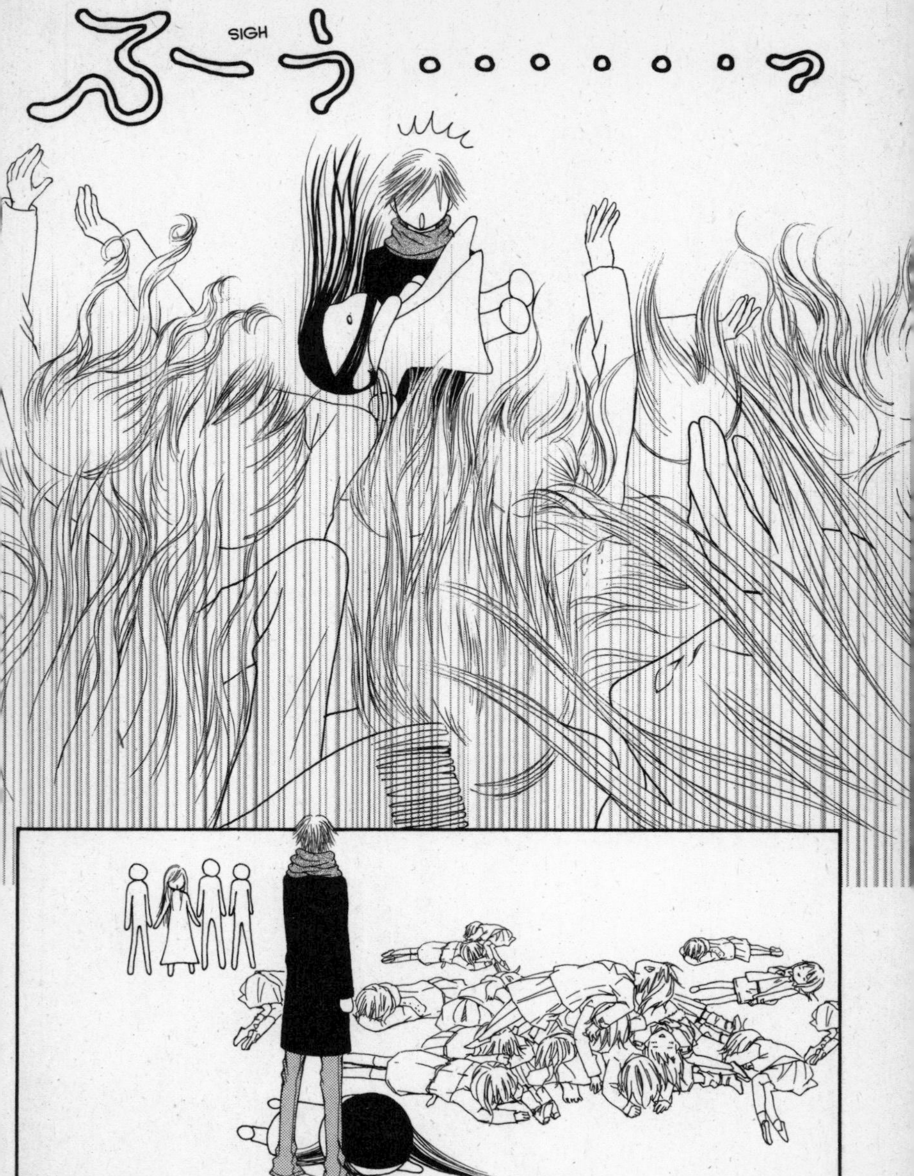
ふ～う・・・・・・っ
SIGH

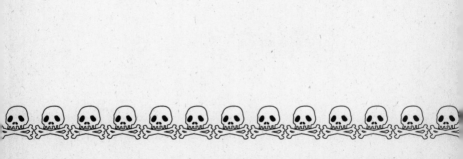

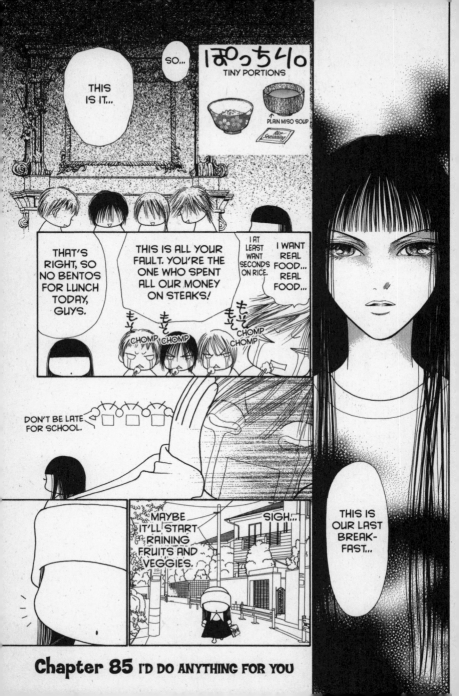

SO...

THIS IS IT...

ぽっち40
TINY PORTIONS

↑ PLAIN MISO SOUP

Rice Seasoning

THAT'S RIGHT, SO NO BENTOS FOR LUNCH TODAY, GUYS.

THIS IS ALL YOUR FAULT. YOU'RE THE ONE WHO SPENT ALL OUR MONEY ON STEAKS!

I AT LEAST WANT SECONDS ON RICE.

I WANT REAL FOOD... REAL FOOD...

CHOMP CHOMP

CHOMP CHOMP

DON'T BE LATE FOR SCHOOL.

MAYBE IT'LL START RAINING FRUITS AND VEGGIES.

SIGH...

THIS IS OUR LAST BREAK-FAST...

Chapter 85 I'D DO ANYTHING FOR YOU

Chapter 85
I'D DO ANYTHING FOR YOU

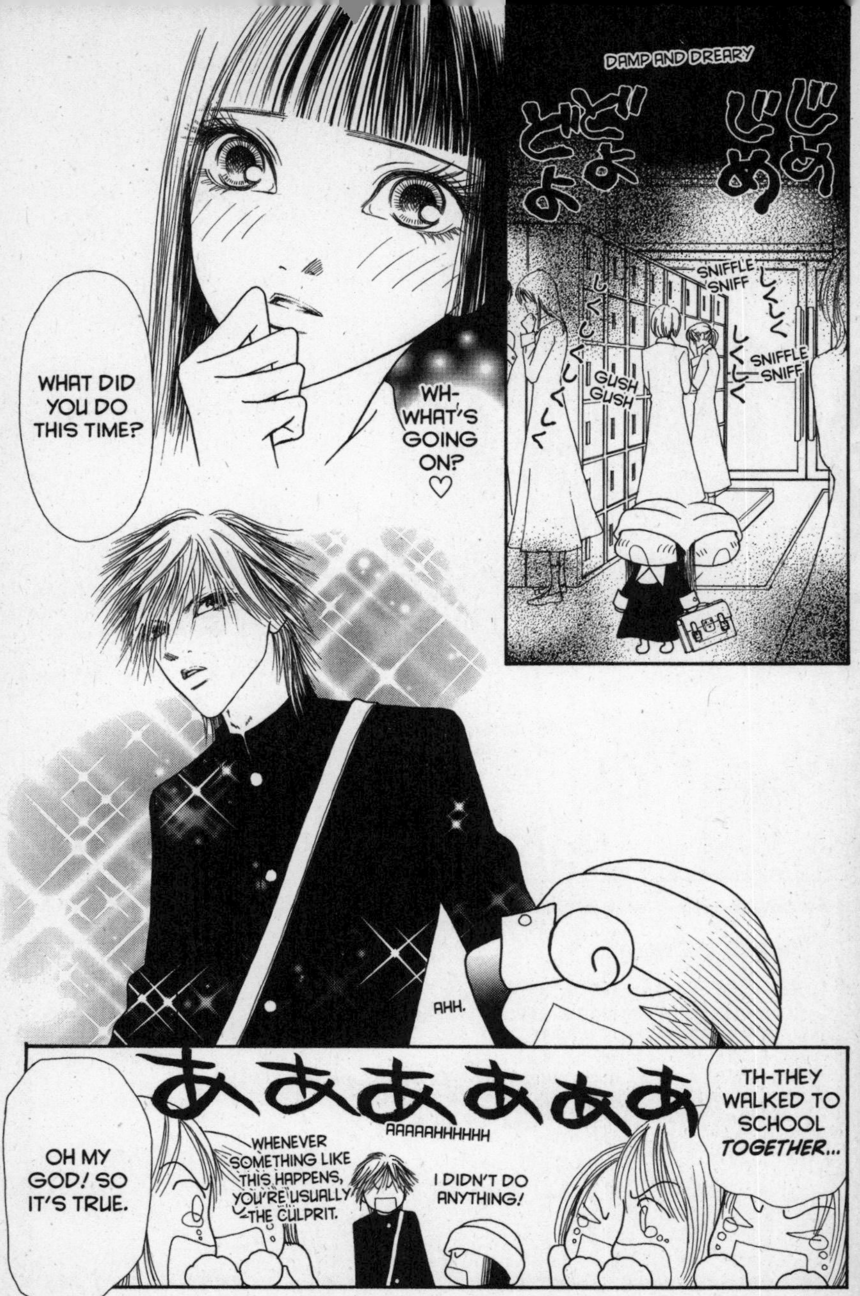
じめじめ
どよどよ
DAMP AND DREARY
しくしくしくしく
SNIFFLE SNIFF
SNIFFLE SNIFF
GUSH GUSH
しくしくしくしく
WH- WHAT'S GOING ON? ♡
WHAT DID YOU DO THIS TIME?
AHH.
TH-THEY WALKED TO SCHOOL *TOGETHER*...
ああああああ
AAAAAHHHHHH
I DIDN'T DO ANYTHING!
WHENEVER SOMETHING LIKE THIS HAPPENS, YOU'RE USUALLY THE CULPRIT.
OH MY GOD! SO IT'S TRUE.

THEY REALLY ARE GOING OUT.

WAAHH

KYOHEI-KUN IS PROTECTING NAKAHARA-SAN.

LOOK HOW HE TRIED TO PROTECT HER...

AAAHHH

NO WE AREN'T!

WHY ARE THEY SAYING THAT?

BEHIND THE SCENES

MY WORK DRAMA FINALLY ENDED! ♥ ♥ ♥

WITH ALL THAT STRESS GONE, I WAS ABLE TO WORK IN PEACE. I WAS REALLY BUSY, BUT "BUSY" AND "DRAMA" ARE TWO TOTALLY DIFFERENT THINGS. ♥

I PUT MY HEAD EDITOR THROUGH A LOT OF TROUBLE. I'M REALLY SORRY. IT WAS REALLY A TERRIBLE TIME. IF I HADN'T GOTTEN TO GO TO ALL THOSE CONCERTS, I MIGHT NOT HAVE SURVIVED. THANKS, EVERYBODY. YOU GUYS ARE THE ONES WHO MAKE THIS FUN.

...IS FIGHTING FOR KYOHEI?

SUNAKO-CHAN...

SHE REFUSES TO LET ANOTHER WOMAN TAKE HER MAN AWAY.

あああああ
AAAAHHH

THAT'S RIGHT.

WHATEVER, JUST LEAVE ME ALONE.

GRUMBLE

きゅるるる
RUMBLE

あああああああ
AAAAHHH

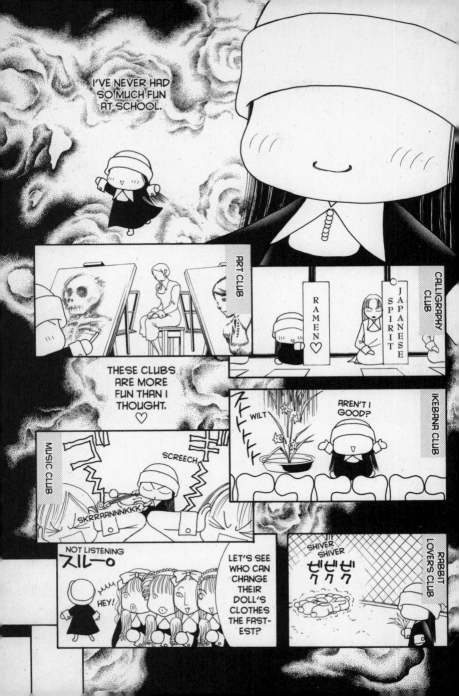

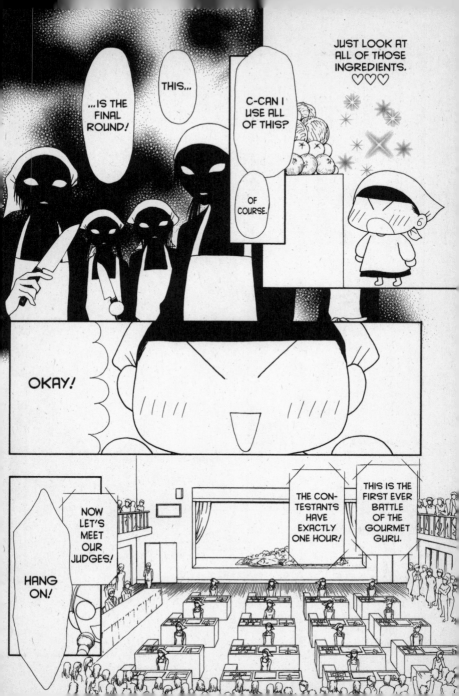

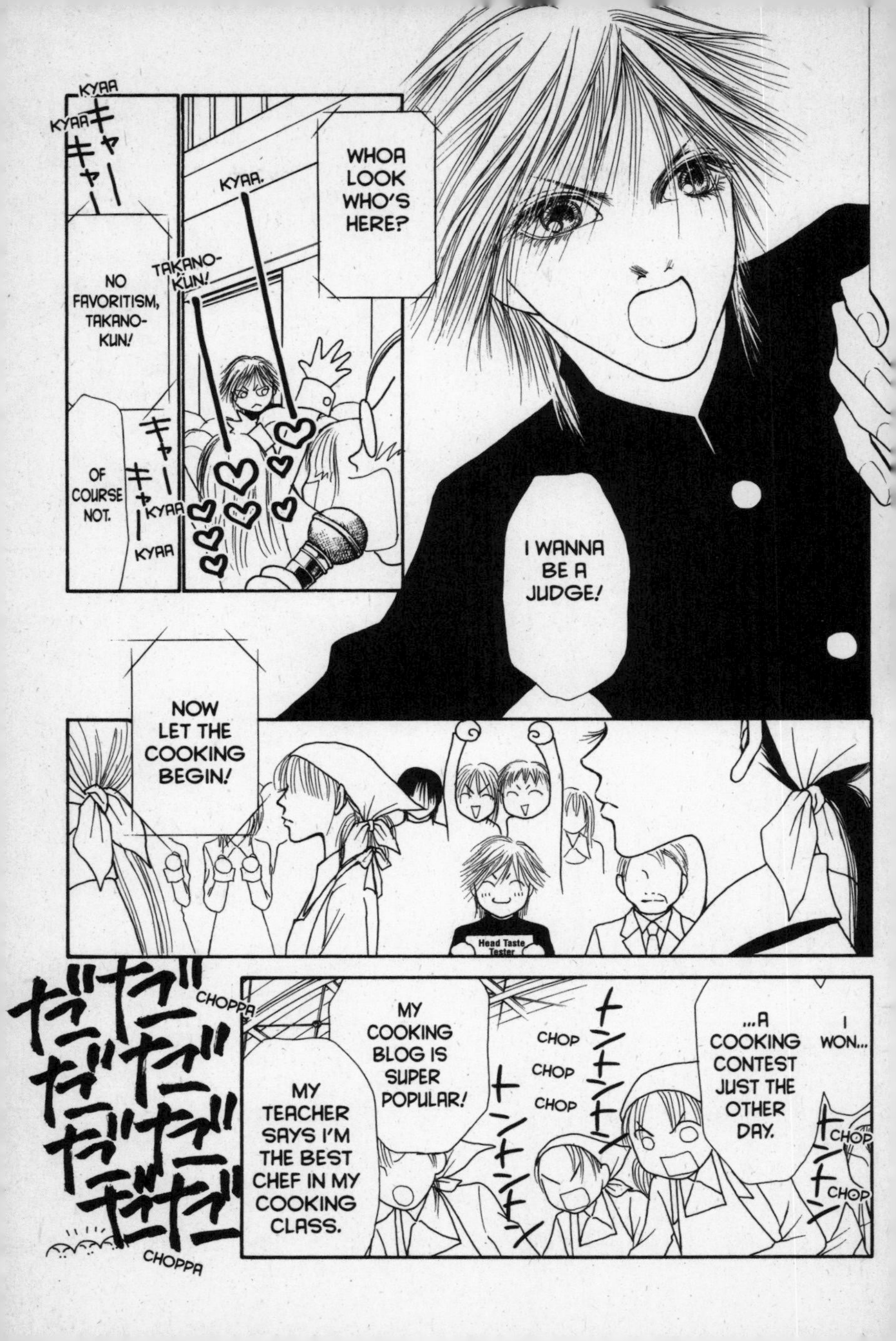
WHOA LOOK WHO'S HERE?
I WANNA BE A JUDGE!
KYAA.
TAKANO-KUN!
KYAA
KYAA
KYAA
NO FAVORITISM, TAKANO-KUN!
OF COURSE NOT.
KYAA
NOW LET THE COOKING BEGIN!
Head Taste Tester
CHOP
CHOP
I WON...
...A COOKING CONTEST JUST THE OTHER DAY.
CHOP
CHOP
CHOP
MY COOKING BLOG IS SUPER POPULAR!
MY TEACHER SAYS I'M THE BEST CHEF IN MY COOKING CLASS.
CHOPPA
CHOPPA

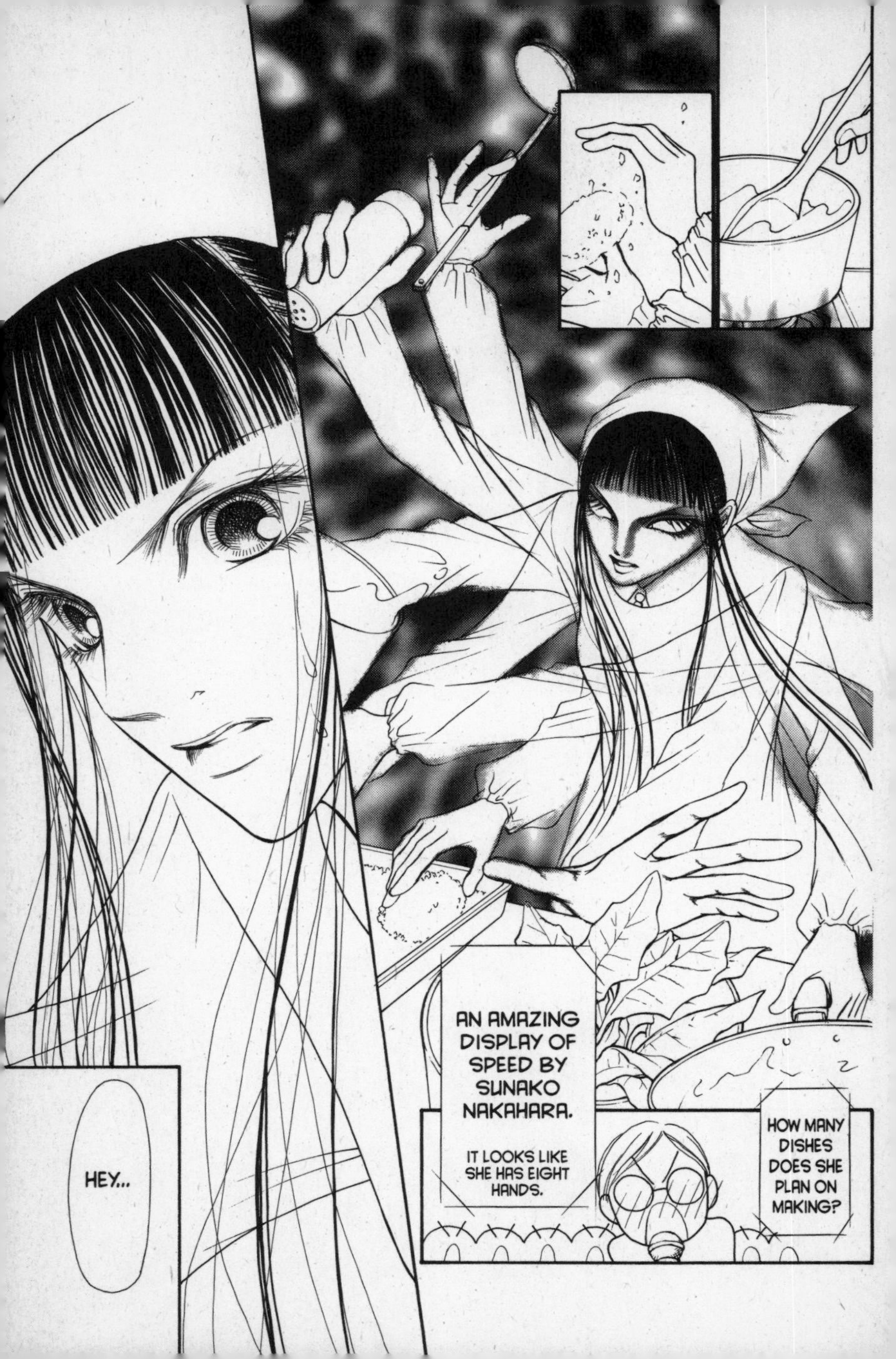
AN AMAZING DISPLAY OF SPEED BY SUNAKO NAKAHARA.
HOW MANY DISHES DOES SHE PLAN ON MAKING?
IT LOOKS LIKE SHE HAS EIGHT HANDS.
HEY...

MMM...

NOT BAD.

CHOMP

K-KYOHEI...

I'LL HAVE THIS ONE TOO.

WOBBLE

YOINK

TAKANO-KUN!

NO SNACKING!

DON'T COME OVER HERE!

CHOMP

CHOMP

CHOMP

WOBBLE

WOBBLE

WOBBLE

WOBBLE

KYOHEI-KUN ACTUALLY ATE MY COOKING...

KYOHEI-KUN...

WH-WHAT'S WRONG, RYO-CHAN?

GUSH

I-I GIVE UP.

THAT WAS ENOUGH FOR ME...

TIME!

YEAH.

SO LET'S HANG IN THERE.

Y-YOU'RE RIGHT.

IF YOU WIN, HE COULD END UP EATING YOUR COOKING EVERY DAY!

DON'T GIVE UP!

ROAR

ROAR

YOU'RE ONLY EATING THE MEAT AND THE FISH.

HUH? TAKANO-KUN.

IT'S GONNA BE HARD TO PICK A WINNER.

ANY ONE OF YOU WOULD MAKE A PERFECT BRIDE.

HA, HA, HA.

THEY'RE ALL VERY DELICIOUS.

WELL, YOU'RE QUITE THE PICKY EATER, KYOHEI TAKANO!

I PRETTY MUCH HATE ALL VEGGIES.

AND I REALLY HATE CARROTS.

I HATE GREENS.

CHOMP CHOMP

DON'T WORRY. I WAS WATCHING, AND...

SHE USED A TON OF VEGGIES.

NAKAHARA-SAN KNOWS EXACTLY WHAT KYOHEI-KUN LIKES!

OH NO!

WHAT SHOULD WE DO?

CARROTS, BELL PEPPERS, CELERY, SPINACH, AND EVEN KOMATSUNA GREENS.

CHOMP

SUNAKO NAKAHARA WHIPPED UP A WHOPPING 10 DISHES.

AND IT LOOKS LIKE SHE DIDN'T TAKE NUTRITIONAL BALANCE INTO CONSIDERATION AT ALL!

AND NOW TAKANO-KUN IS STANDING BEFORE NAKAHARA-SAN'S DISHES.

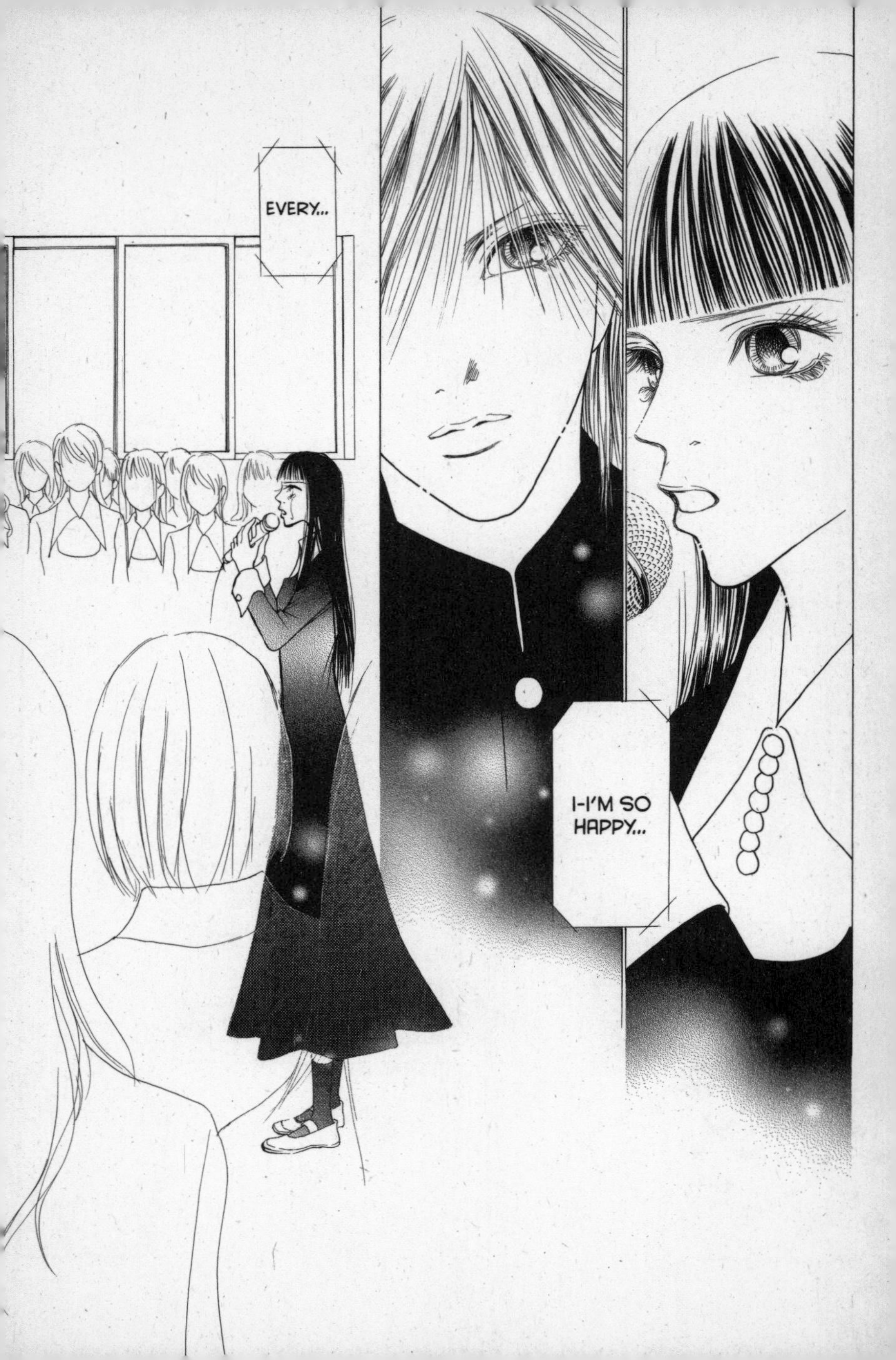
I-I'M SO HAPPY...
EVERY...

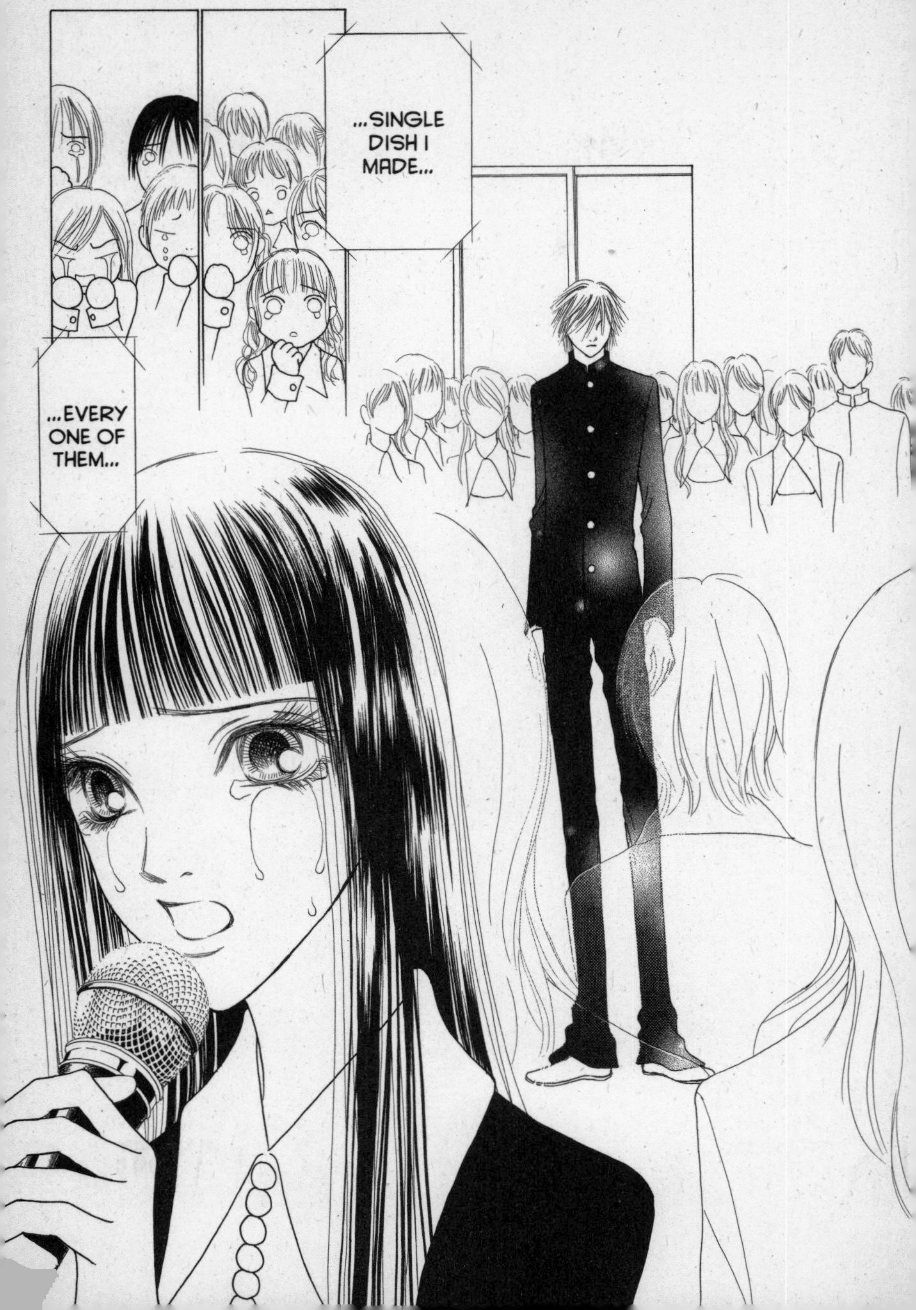
...SINGLE DISH I MADE...
...EVERY ONE OF THEM...

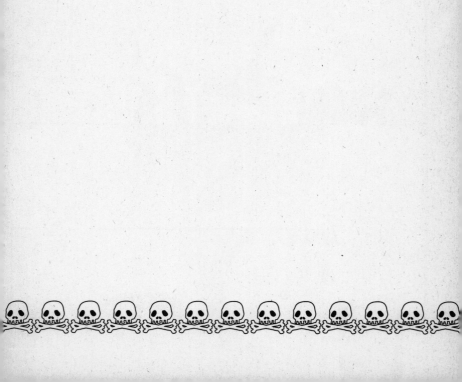

Chapter 86 LOVE IS A ONE-WAY STREET

Chapter 86
LOVE IS A ONE-WAY STREET

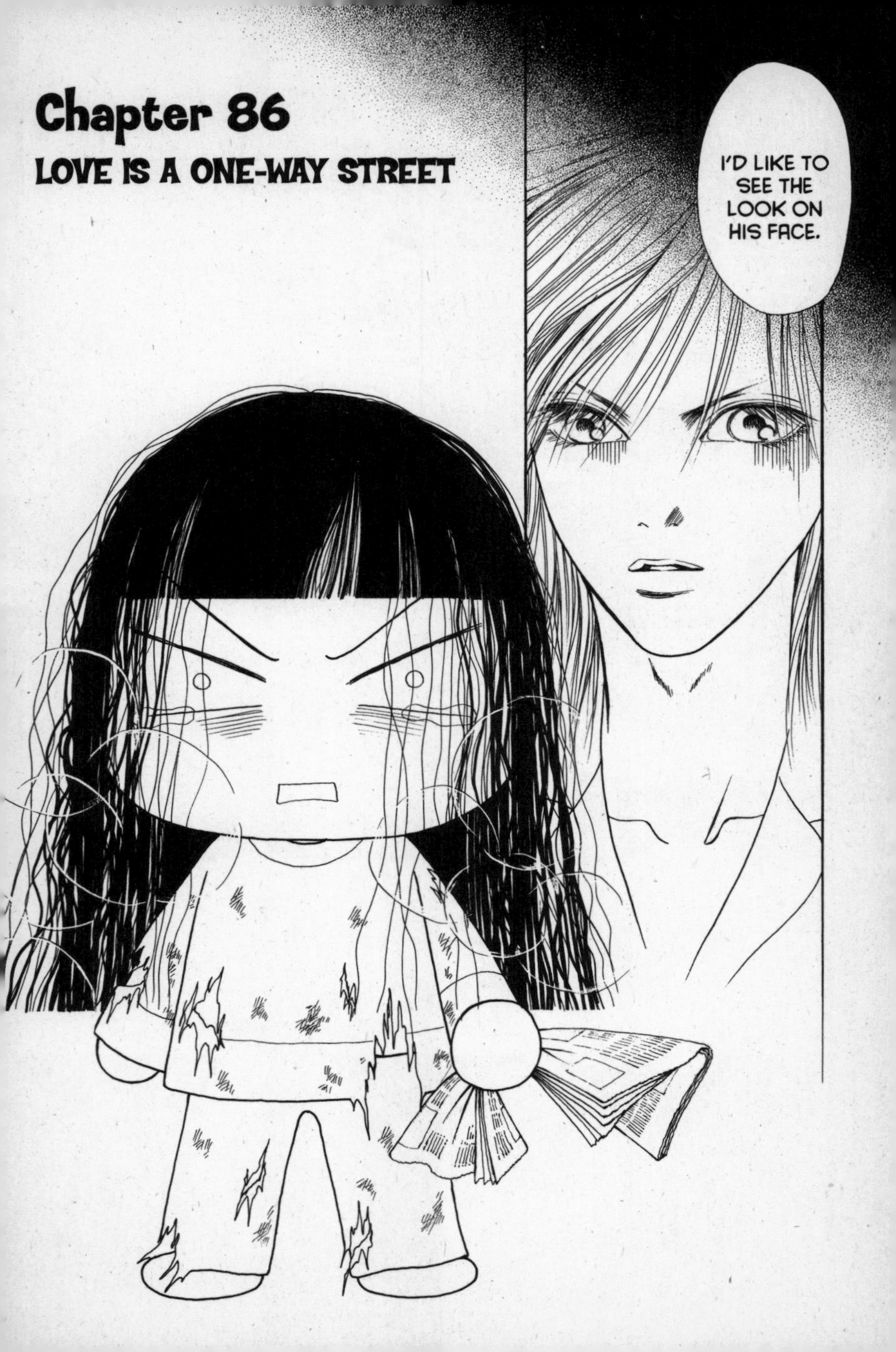
I'D LIKE TO SEE THE LOOK ON HIS FACE.

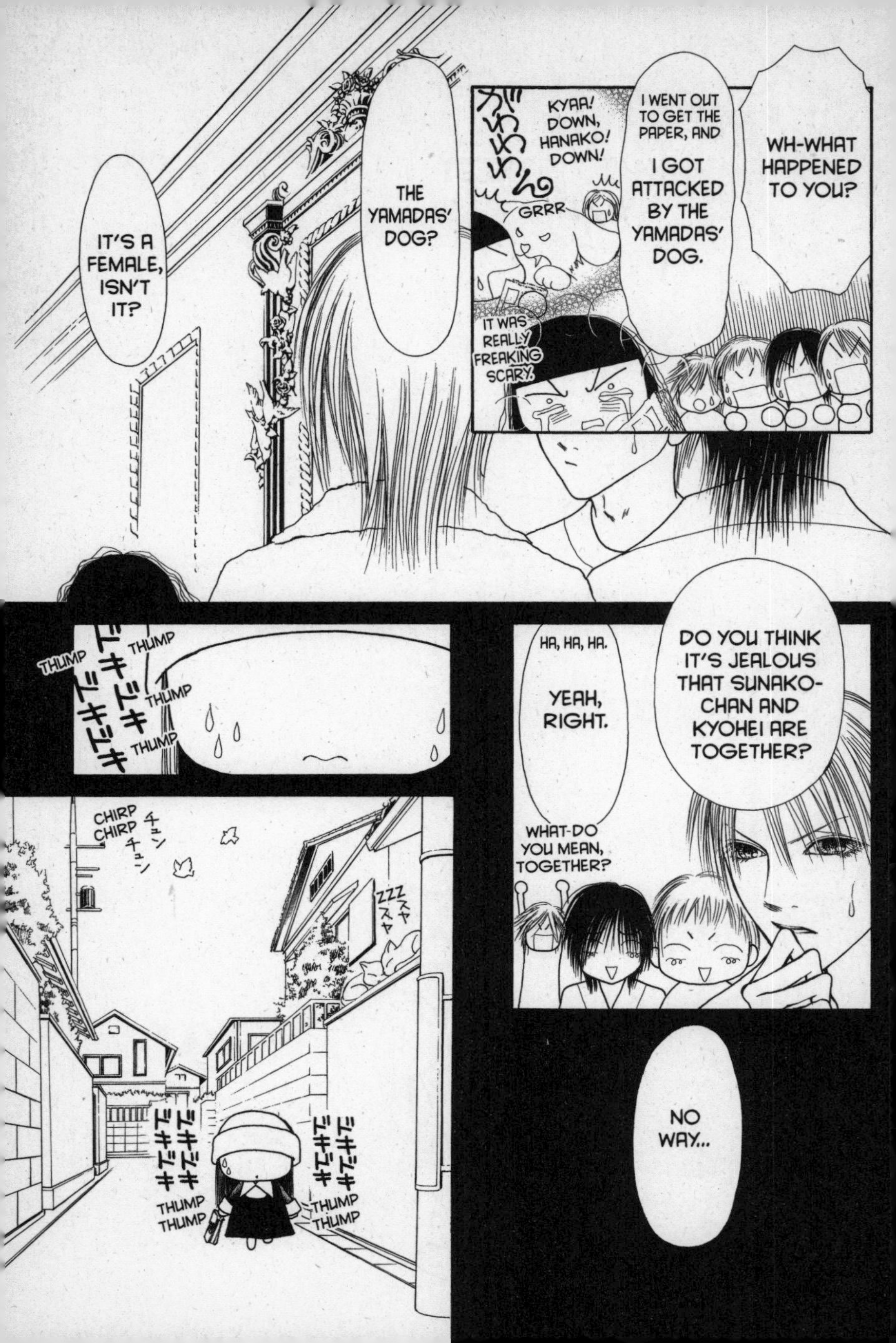
WH-WHAT HAPPENED TO YOU?
I WENT OUT TO GET THE PAPER, AND I GOT ATTACKED BY THE YAMADAS' DOG.
KYAA! DOWN, HANAKO! DOWN!
GRRR
IT WAS REALLY FREAKING SCARY.
THE YAMADAS' DOG?
IT'S A FEMALE, ISN'T IT?
DO YOU THINK IT'S JEALOUS THAT SUNAKO-CHAN AND KYOHEI ARE TOGETHER?
HA, HA, HA.
YEAH, RIGHT.
WHAT-DO YOU MEAN, TOGETHER?
NO WAY...
ドキドキドキドキ
THUMP THUMP THUMP THUMP
チュンチュン
CHIRP CHIRP
スヤスヤ
ZZZ
ドキドキドキドキ
THUMP THUMP
ドキドキドキドキ
THUMP THUMP

RANMARU WAS EXACTLY RIGHT.

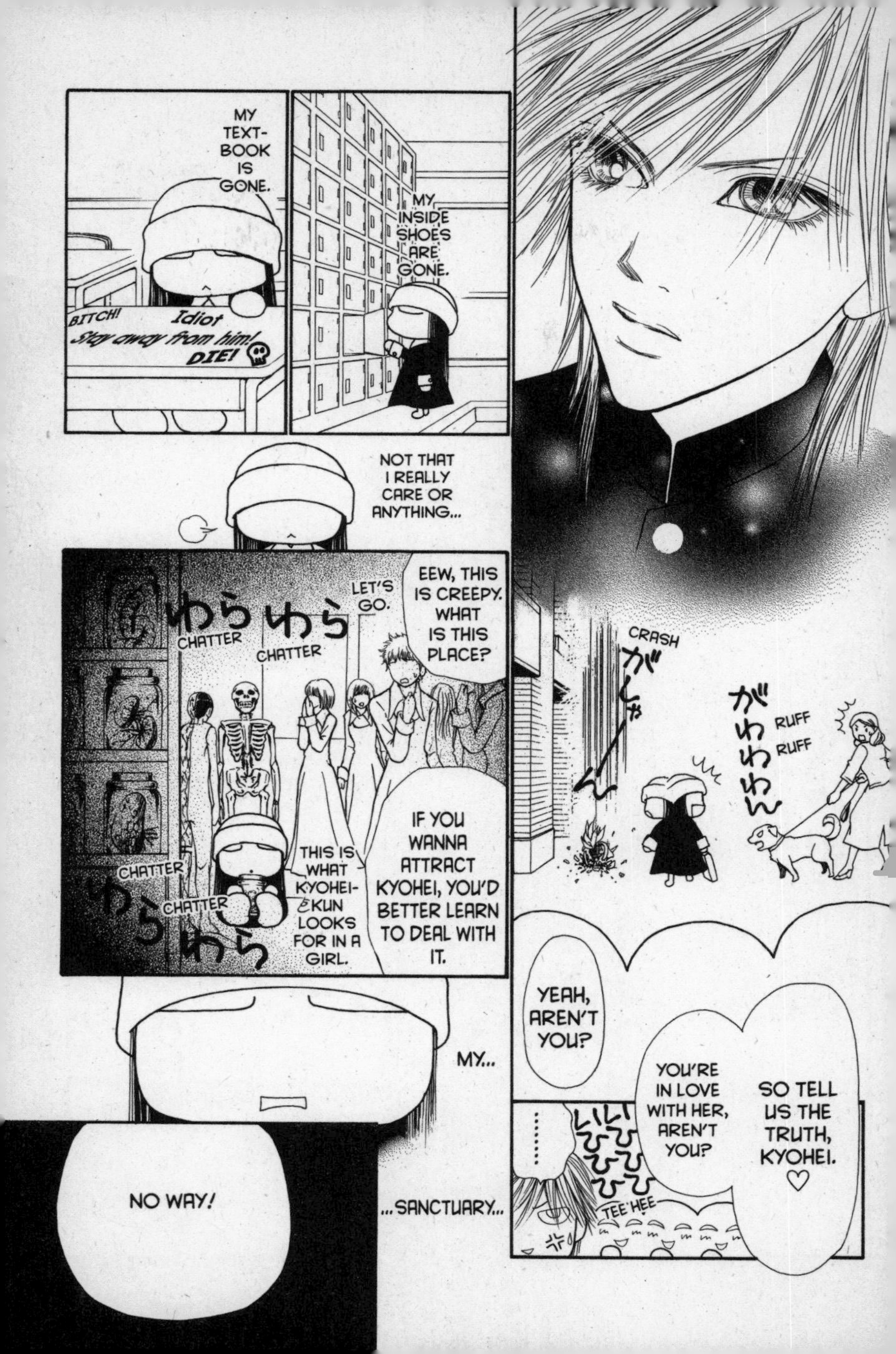
CRASH
がしゃーん
がわわわん
RUFF RUFF
SO TELL US THE TRUTH, KYOHEI. ♥
YOU'RE IN LOVE WITH HER, AREN'T YOU?
YEAH, AREN'T YOU?
......
TEE HEE
MY INSIDE SHOES ARE GONE.
MY TEXT-BOOK IS GONE.
BITCH! Idiot Stay away from him! DIE!
NOT THAT I REALLY CARE OR ANYTHING...
EEW, THIS IS CREEPY. WHAT IS THIS PLACE?
LET'S GO.
わら わら
CHATTER CHATTER
IF YOU WANNA ATTRACT KYOHEI, YOU'D BETTER LEARN TO DEAL WITH IT.
THIS IS WHAT KYOHEI-KUN LOOKS FOR IN A GIRL.
CHATTER CHATTER
わら わら
MY...
...SANCTUARY...
NO WAY!

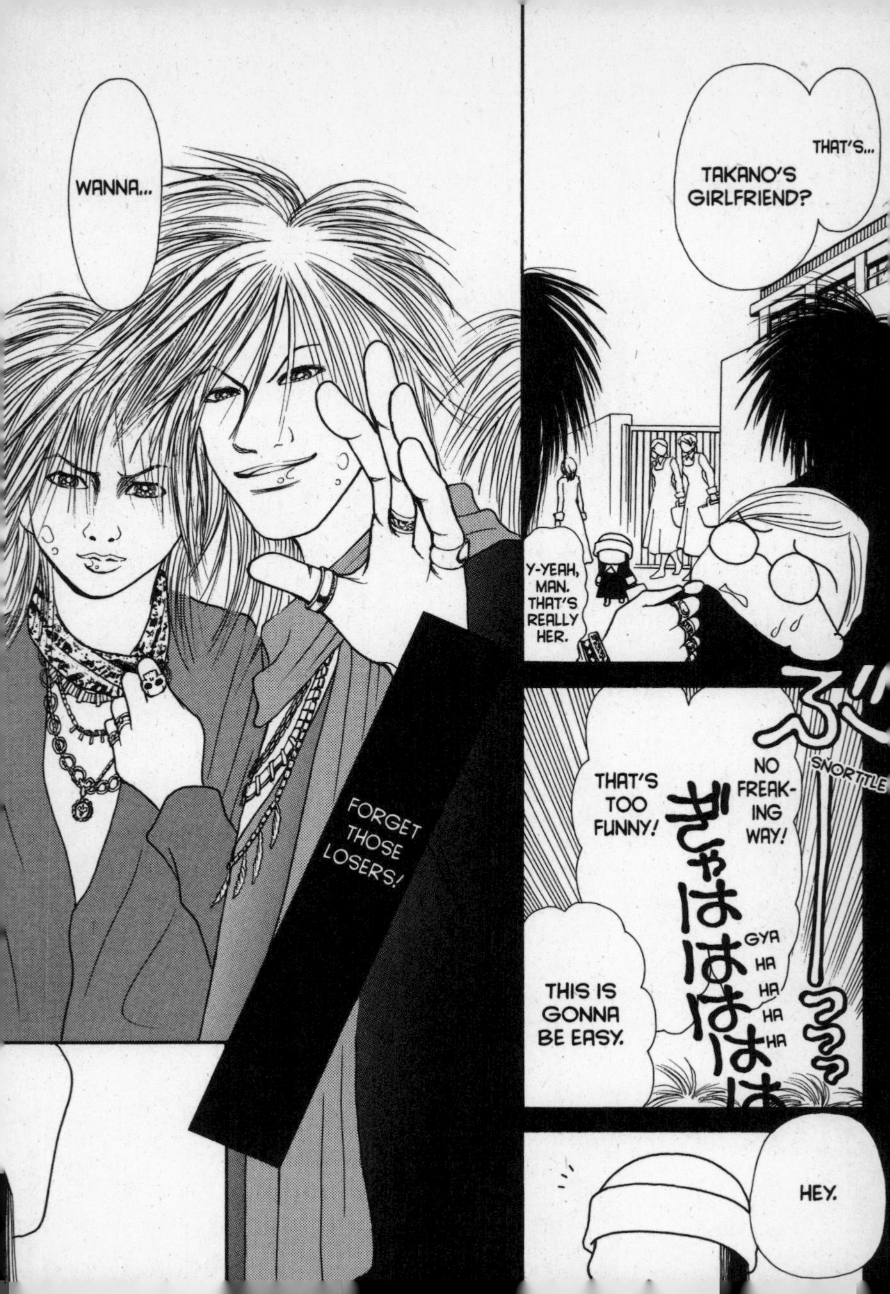
THAT'S... TAKANO'S GIRLFRIEND?
Y-YEAH, MAN. THAT'S REALLY HER.
ぶ
SNORTLE
NO FREAK-ING WAY!
THAT'S TOO FUNNY!
ぎゃははは
GYA HA HA HA HA
THIS IS GONNA BE EASY.
HEY.
WANNA...
FORGET THOSE LOSERS!

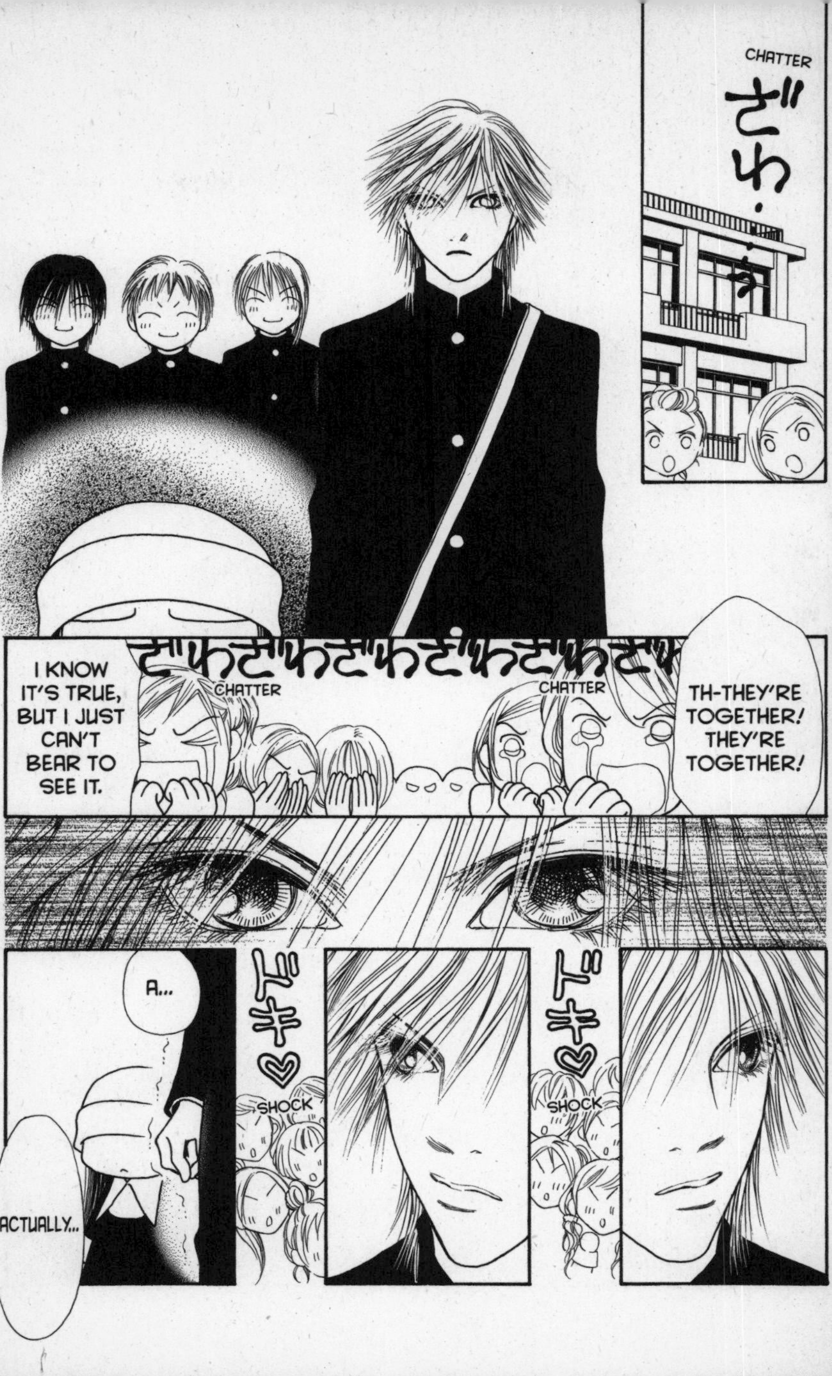
CHATTER
ざわ…
TH-THEY'RE TOGETHER! THEY'RE TOGETHER!
ざわざわざわざわざわ
CHATTER
CHATTER
I KNOW IT'S TRUE, BUT I JUST CAN'T BEAR TO SEE IT.
ドキ♥
SHOCK
ドキ♥
SHOCK
A...
ACTUALLY...

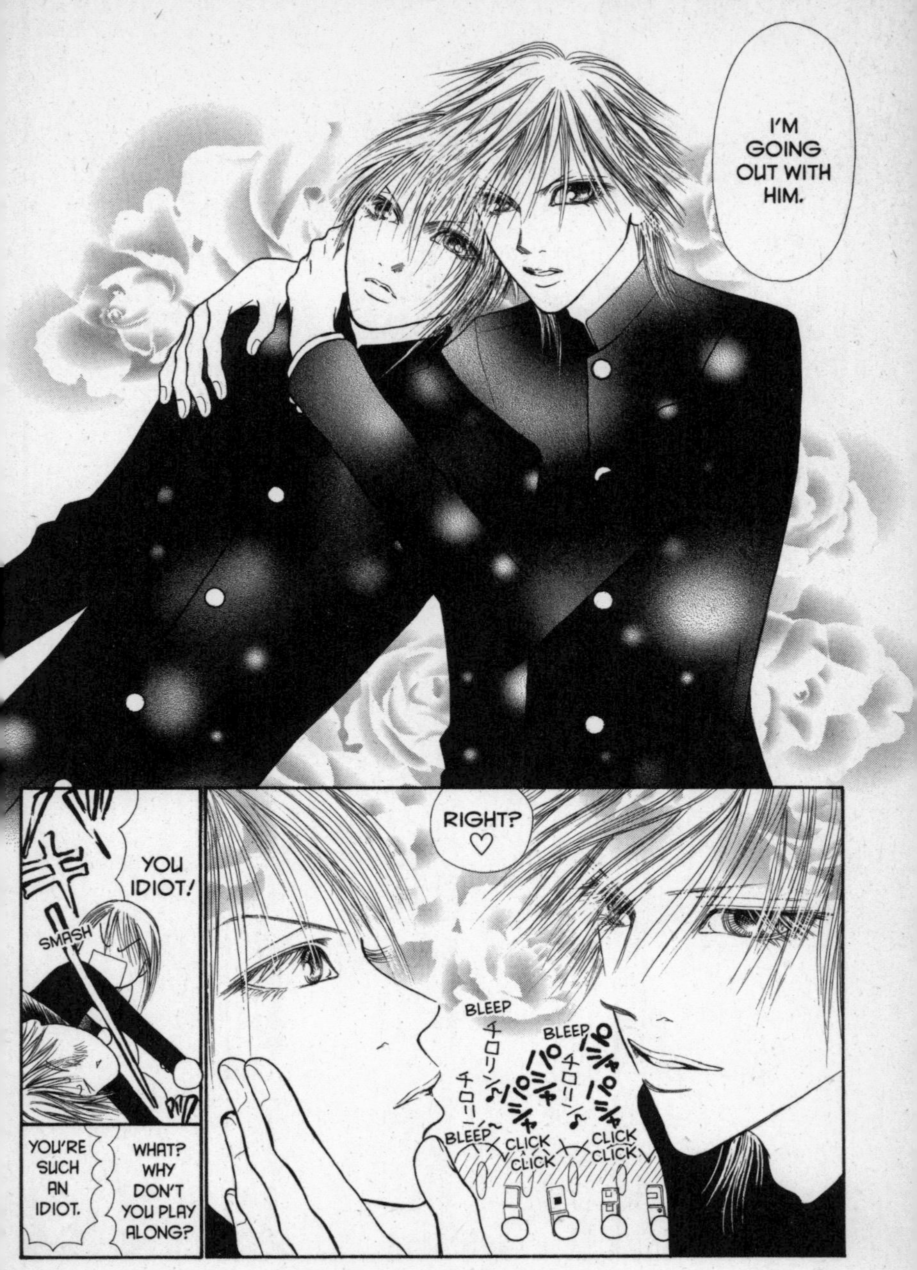

I'M GOING OUT WITH HIM.
RIGHT? ♡
BLEEP
チロリン♪
BLEEP
パシャパシャ
チロリン♪
パシャパシャ
チロリ～
BLEEP
CLICK CLICK
CLICK CLICK
YOU IDIOT!
SMASH
WHAT? WHY DON'T YOU PLAY ALONG?
YOU'RE SUCH AN IDIOT.

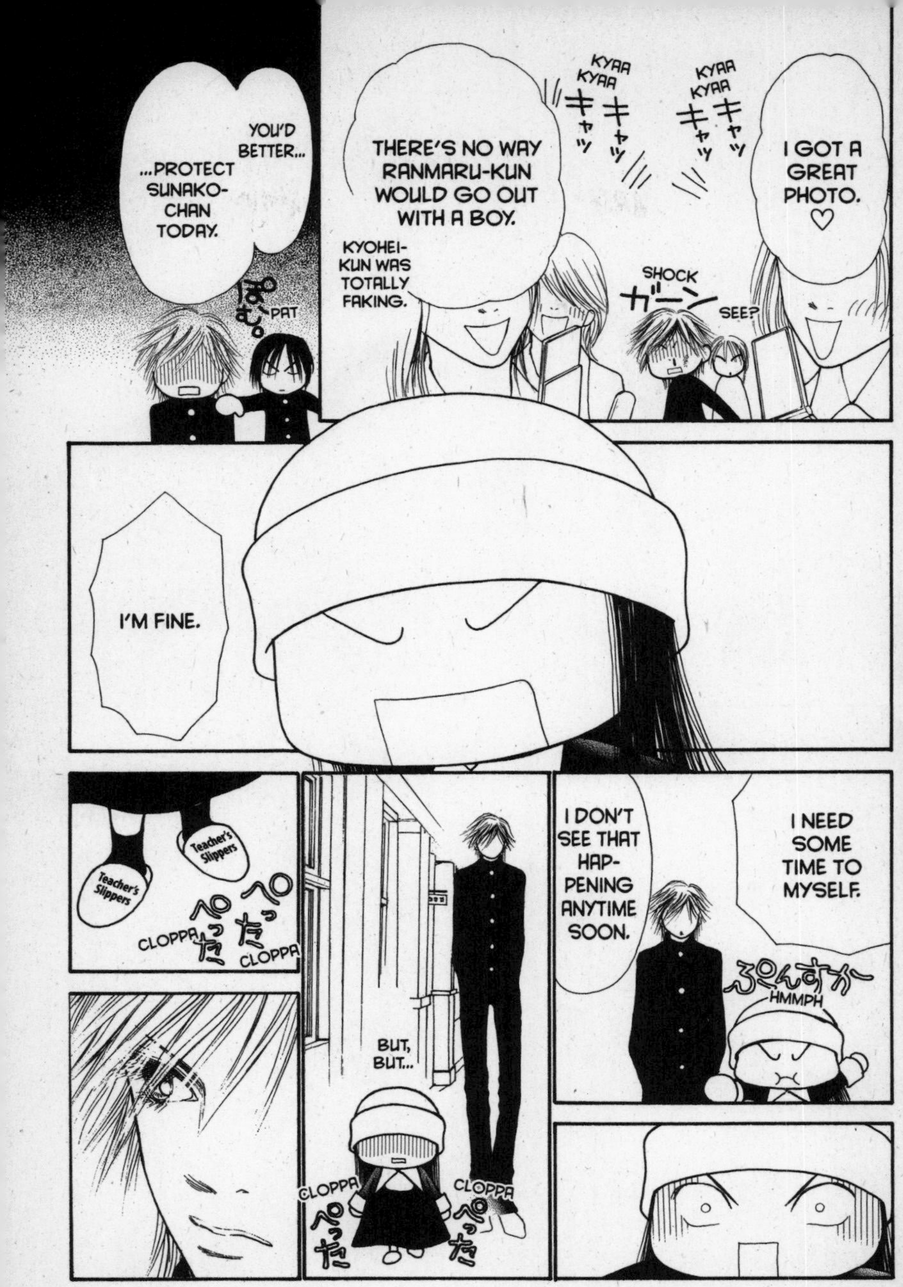
I GOT A GREAT PHOTO. ♡
KYAA KYAA
キャッキャッ
KYAA KYAA
キャッキャッ
SEE?
SHOCK
ガーン
THERE'S NO WAY RANMARU-KUN WOULD GO OUT WITH A BOY.
KYOHEI-KUN WAS TOTALLY FAKING.
YOU'D BETTER...
...PROTECT SUNAKO-CHAN TODAY.
PAT
ぽむ。
I'M FINE.
I NEED SOME TIME TO MYSELF.
I DON'T SEE THAT HAP-PENING ANYTIME SOON.
HMMPH
ぷんすか
BUT, BUT...
CLOPPA
ぺったぺった
CLOPPA
Teacher's Slippers
Teacher's Slippers
CLOPPA
CLOPPA
ぺったぺった

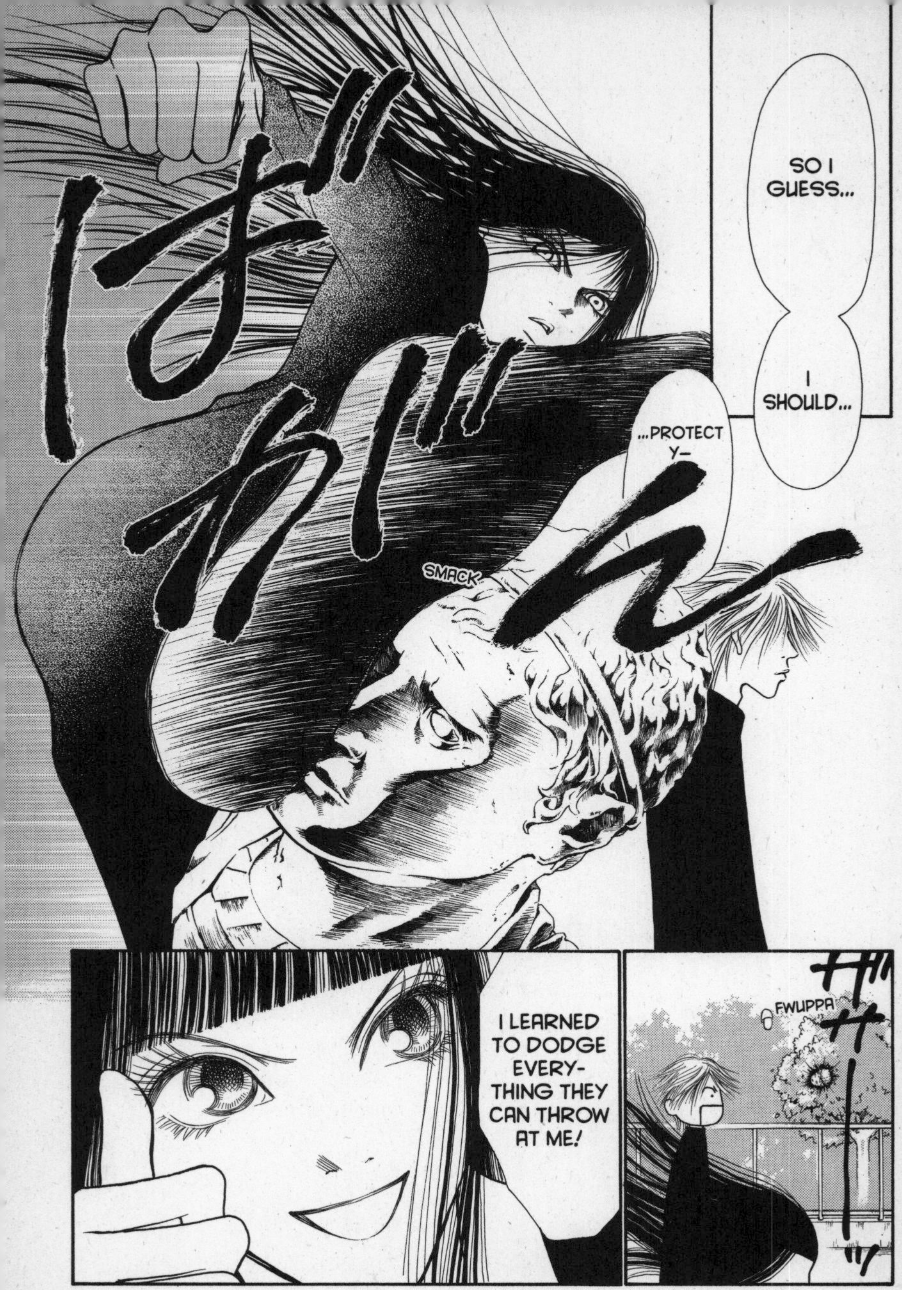
SO I GUESS...
I SHOULD...
...PROTECT Y—
SMACK
FWUPPA
I LEARNED TO DODGE EVERY-THING THEY CAN THROW AT ME!

— 117 —

— 118 —

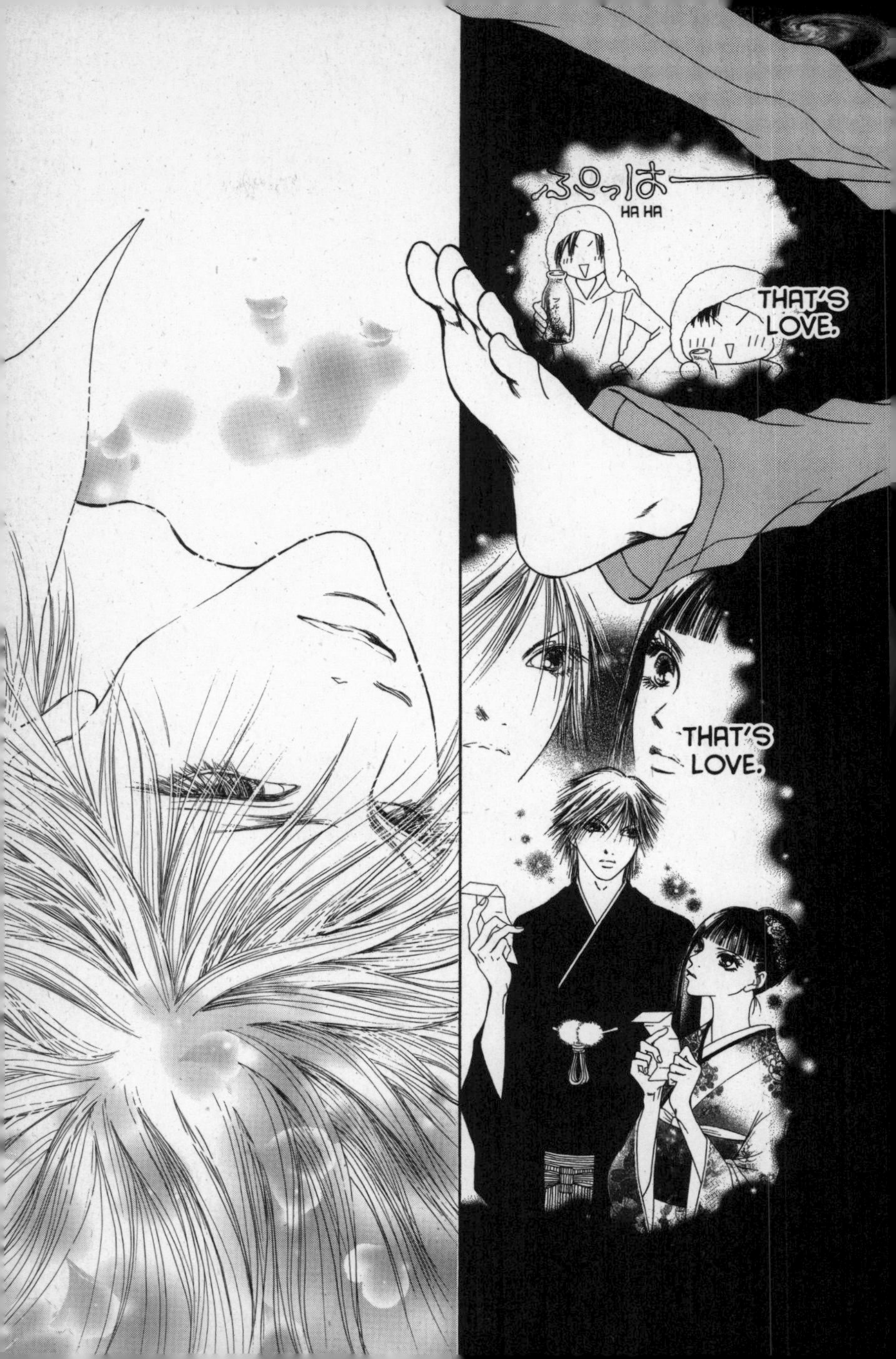
ぷっはー
HA HA
THAT'S LOVE.
THAT'S LOVE.

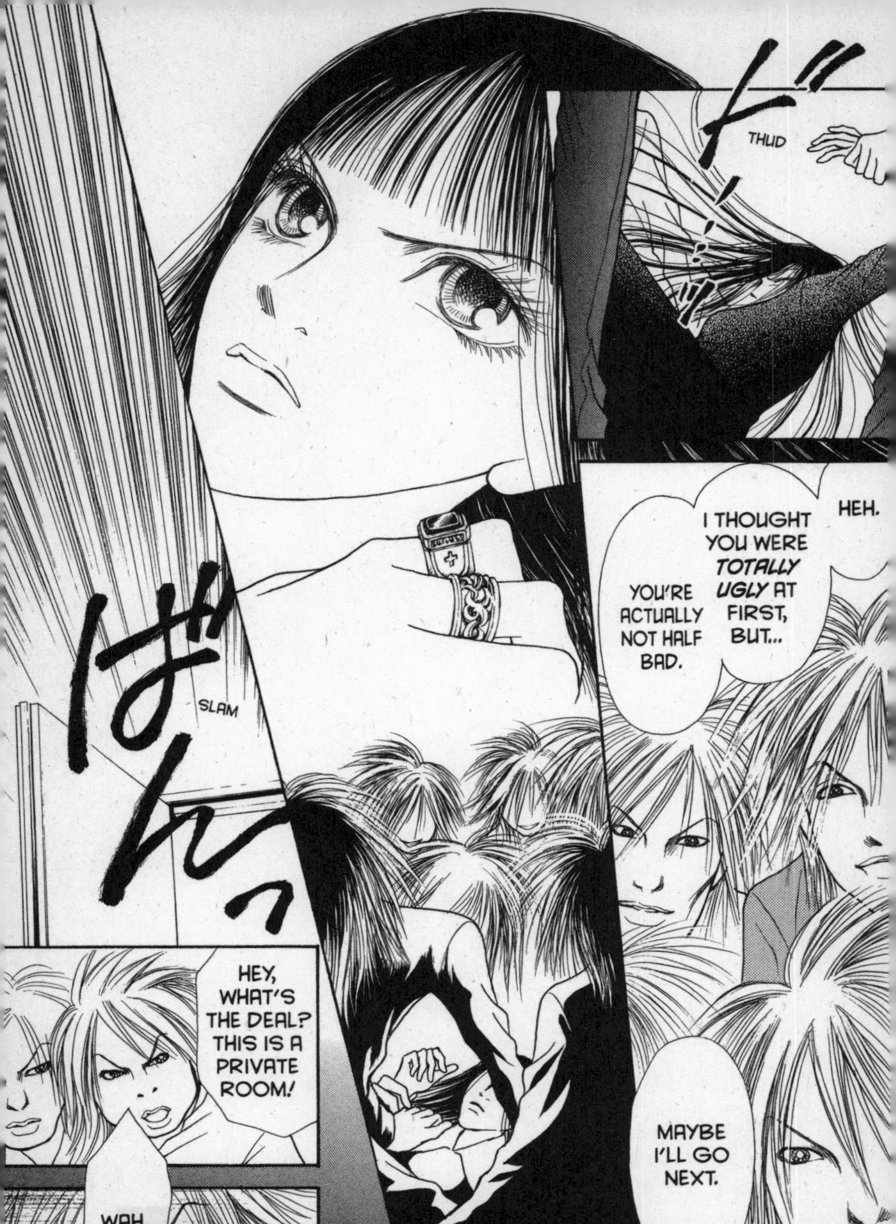
THUD
SLAM
HEH.
I THOUGHT YOU WERE *TOTALLY UGLY* AT FIRST, BUT...
YOU'RE ACTUALLY NOT HALF BAD.
MAYBE I'LL GO NEXT.
HEY, WHAT'S THE DEAL? THIS IS A PRIVATE ROOM!
WAH.

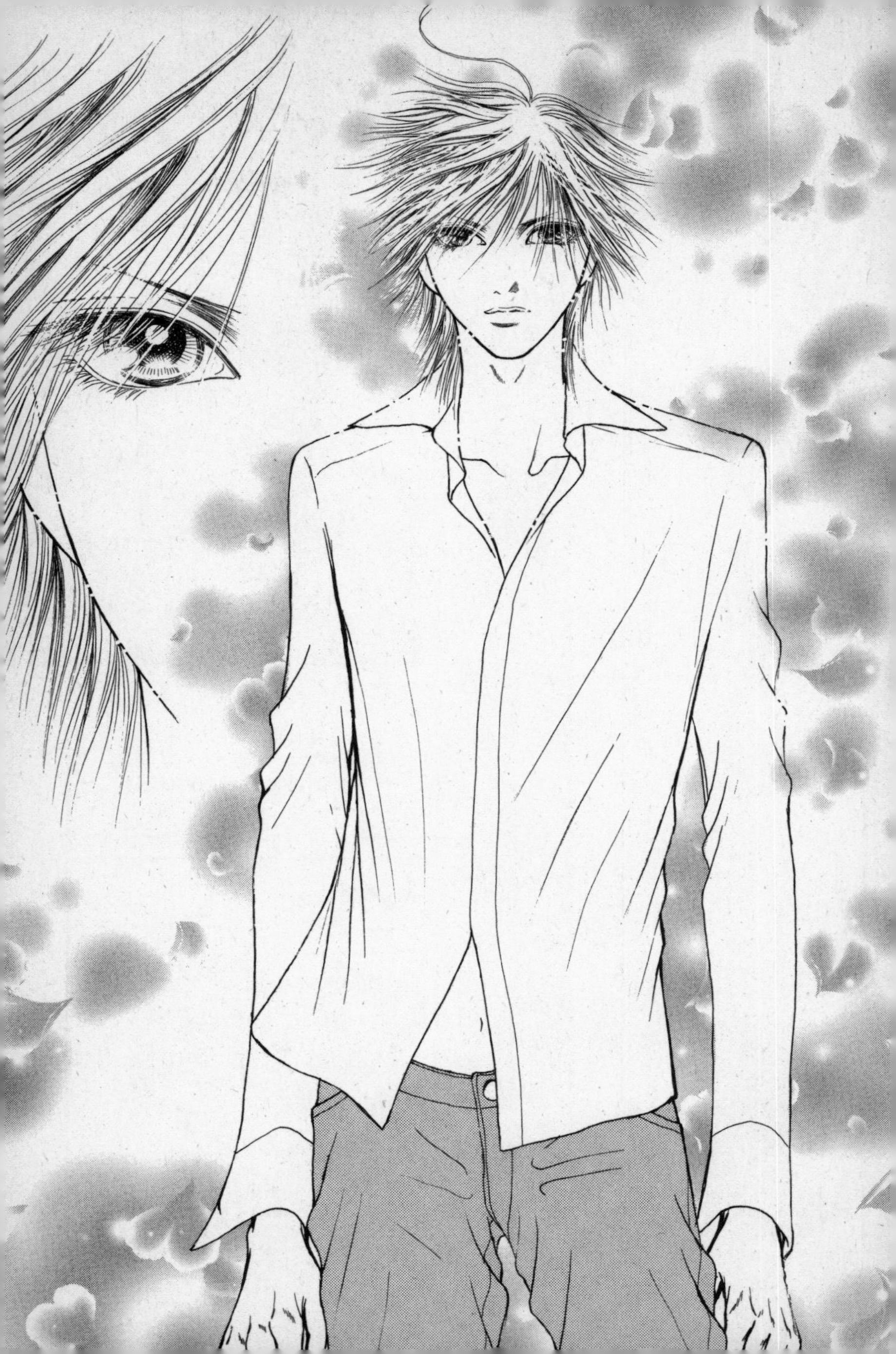

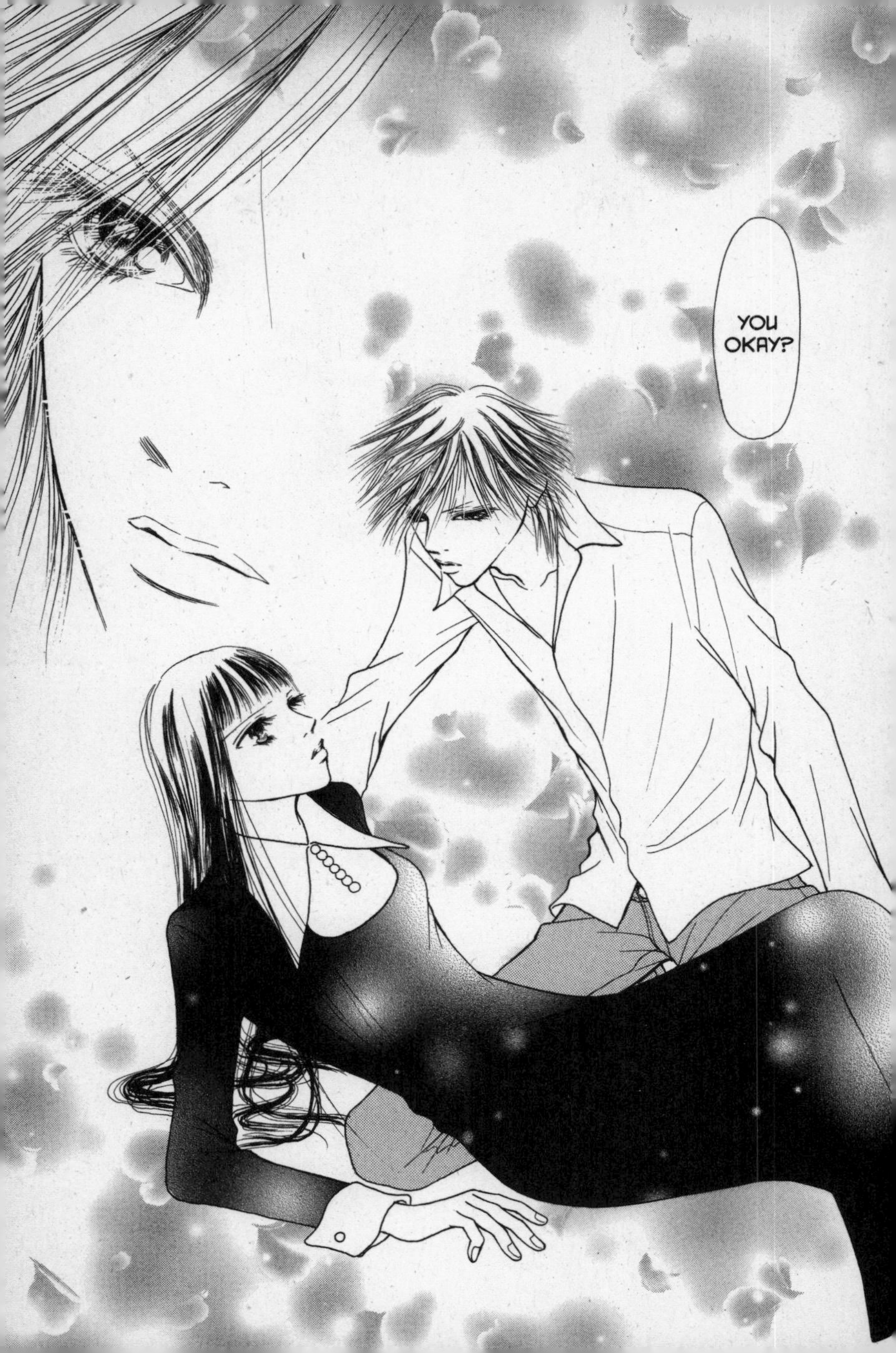
YOU OKAY?

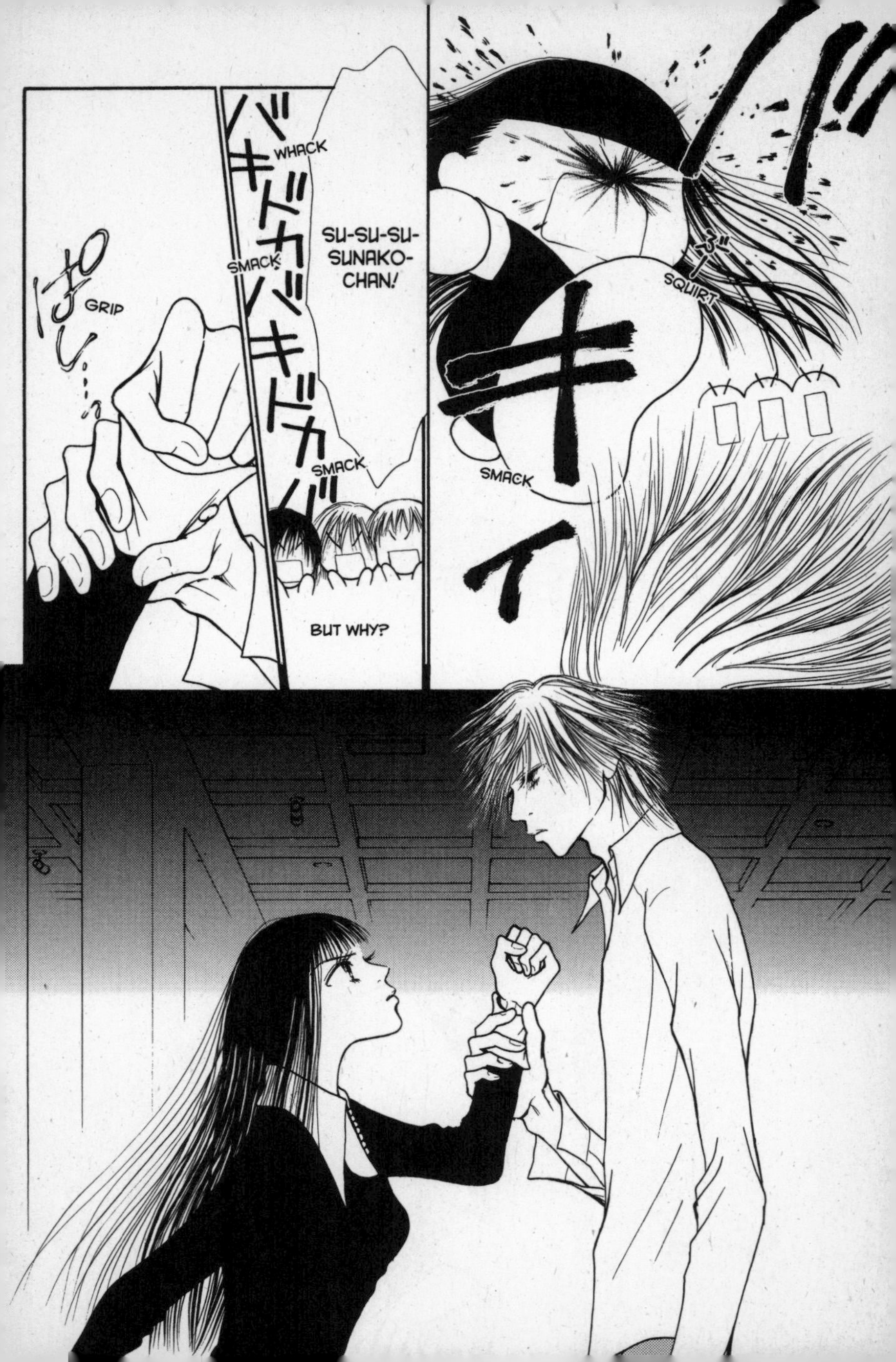
SQUIRT
SMACK
WHACK
SMACK
バキドカバキドカバ
SU-SU-SU-SUNAKO-CHAN!
SMACK
BUT WHY?
GRIP

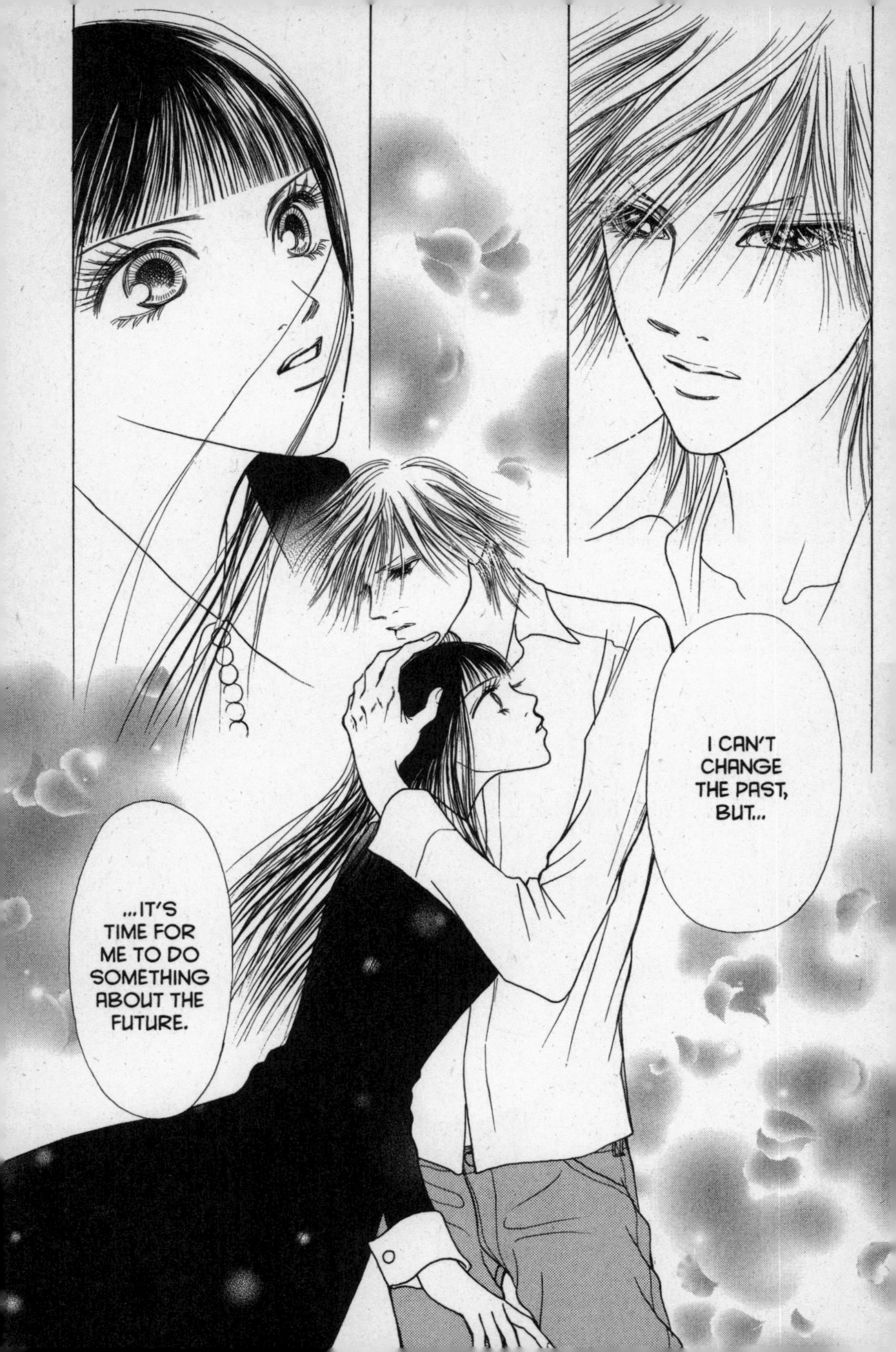
I CAN'T CHANGE THE PAST, BUT...
...IT'S TIME FOR ME TO DO SOMETHING ABOUT THE FUTURE.

GUSH

GUSH

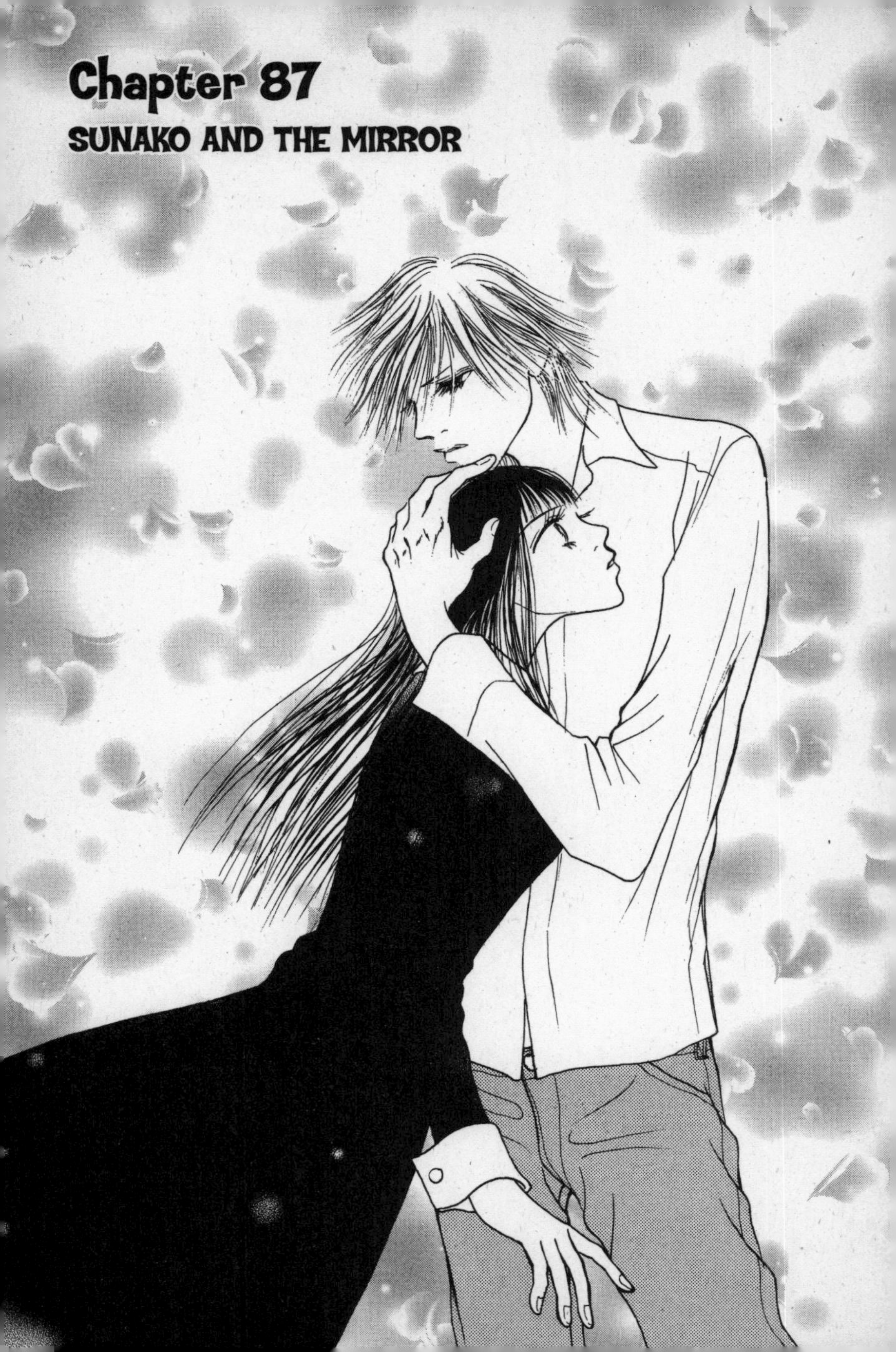
Chapter 87
SUNAKO AND THE MIRROR

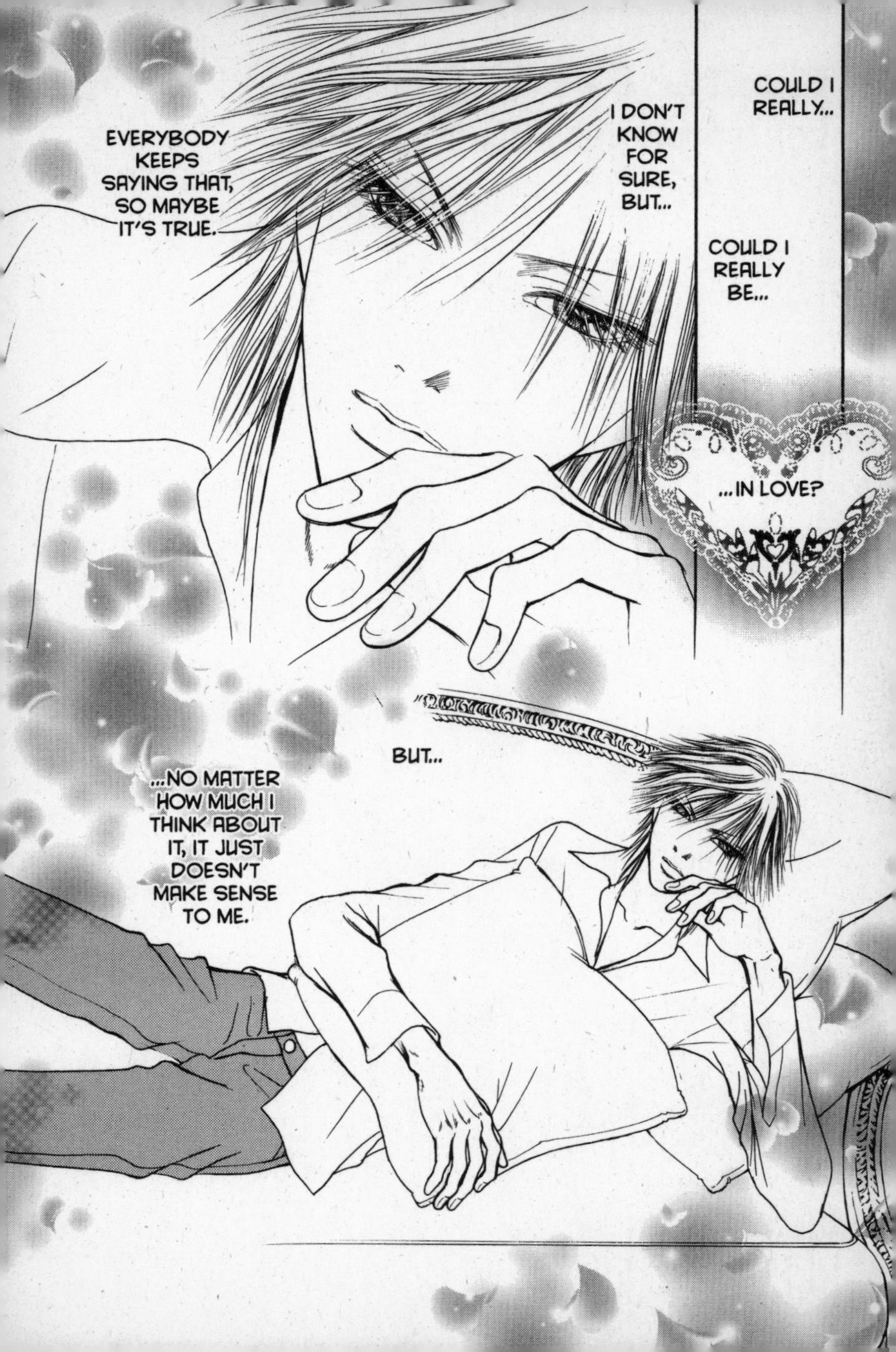
COULD I REALLY...
COULD I REALLY BE...
...IN LOVE?
I DON'T KNOW FOR SURE, BUT...
EVERYBODY KEEPS SAYING THAT, SO MAYBE IT'S TRUE.
BUT...
...NO MATTER HOW MUCH I THINK ABOUT IT, IT JUST DOESN'T MAKE SENSE TO ME.

SPECIAL THANKS

YOUICHIRO TOMITA-SAMA
IYO MORI-SAMA

REN KOIUMI-SAMA
RYO NARUMI-SAMA
YUUKA KITAGAWA-SAMA

INNAN-SAMA
INO-SAMA
HOSOI-SAMA
EDITOR IN CHIEF-SAMA
EVERYBODY IN THE EDITING
DEPARTMENT

MACHIKO SAKURAI
MIZUHO AIMOTO-SENSEI

EVERYBODY WHO'S READING THIS RIGHT NOW♡

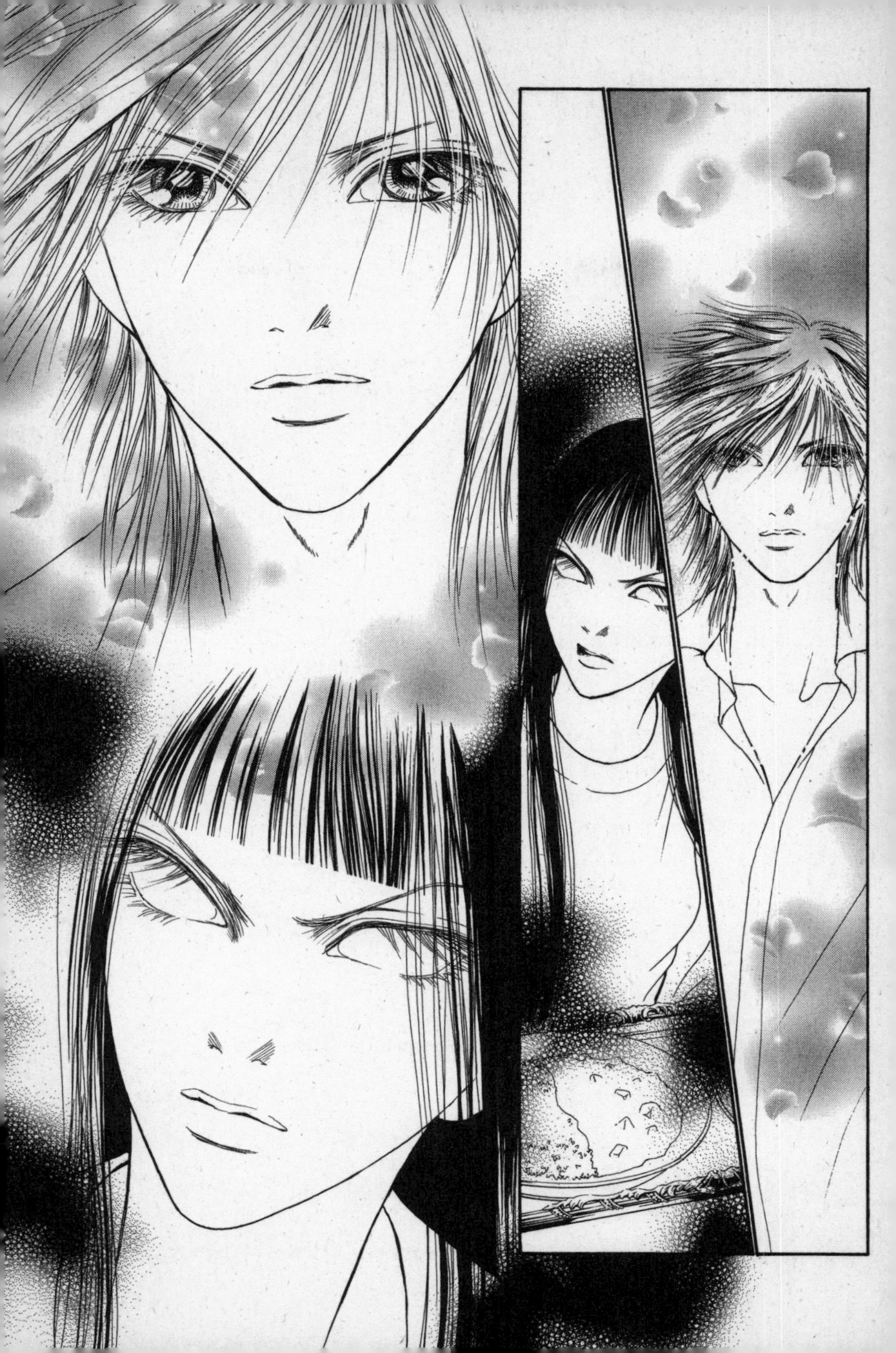

SUNAKO-CHAN HAS NO SELF-CONFIDENCE.

WHY'D YOU MAKE US DO THAT?

YOU KNEW THAT WOULD HAPPEN.

HMMPH!

SHE'S PROBABLY THINKING "THERE'S NO WAY THAT BISHONEN COULD REALLY LIKE ME.

HE'S JUST TEASING ME.

UM, WE DON'T REALLY THINK OF OURSELVES AS HOT BISHONEN.

IF I WAS SUPER HOT, THEN MAYBE, BUT..."

AND THAT'S WHERE THE *THREE OF US* COME IN.

SHE'LL START TO COME AROUND. ♡

IF THREE HOT BISHONEN LIKE US COMPLIMENT HER...

HA.

THINKING ABOUT IT ISN'T GONNA SOLVE ANYTHING.

I THINK THIS IS MORE ABOUT SUNAKO-CHAN JUST TRYING TO AVOID LOVE AT ALL COSTS.

YOU THINK THIS ALL STEMS FROM THE TIME...

BUT I'LL GIVE YOU CREDIT FOR TRYING.

IT'S NO USE, RAN-MARU.

...THAT GUY CALLED SUNAKO-CHAN UGLY, BUT I DON'T KNOW...

WAH

RANMARU JUST LOVES ROMANCE.

IT DOESN'T MATTER IF HE'S INVOLVED OR NOT.

THIS ONE IS SURE TO WORK!

DON'T WORRY, I HAVE ANOTHER PLAN. ♡

TIME TO GET BUSY.

HOP 忙 Hop

BOING BOING

IF I JUST LET GO...

I JUST WANT TO LIVE MY LIFE BY MYSELF.

WHY WON'T EVERYBODY JUST LEAVE ME ALONE?

...MAYBE I'LL FIND MY ANSWER.

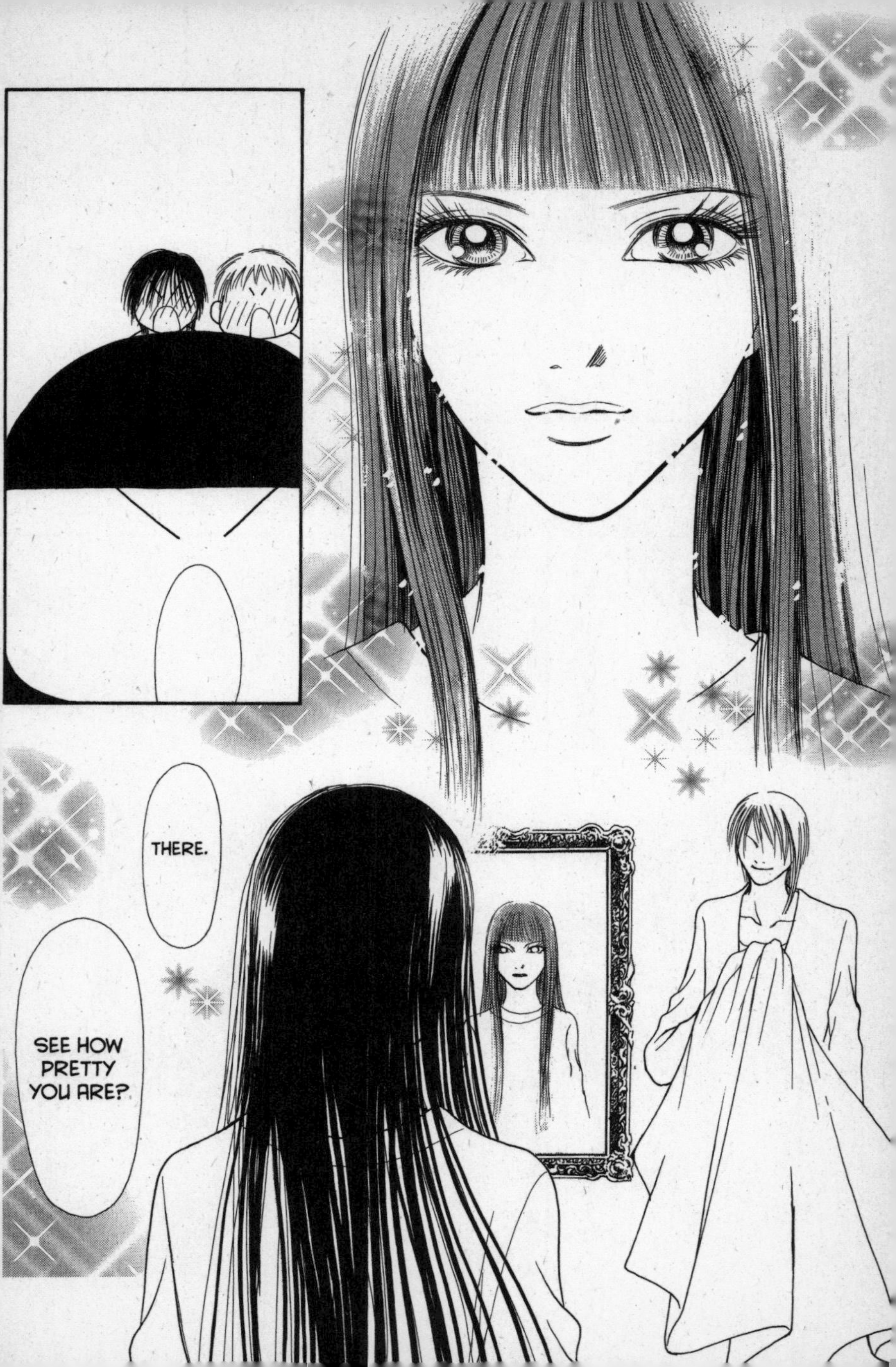
THERE.
SEE HOW PRETTY YOU ARE?

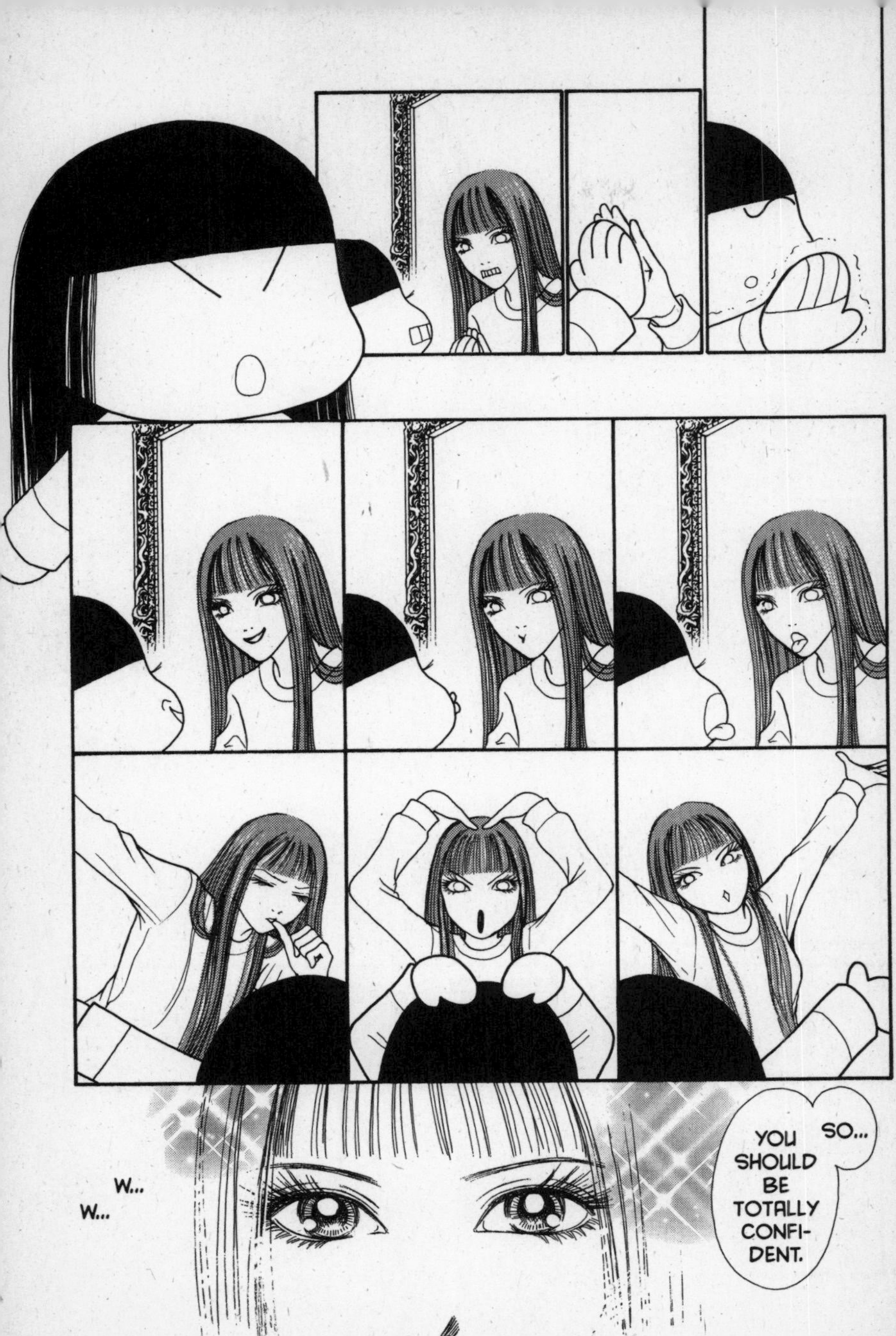
SO...
YOU SHOULD BE TOTALLY CONFI-DENT.
W...
W...

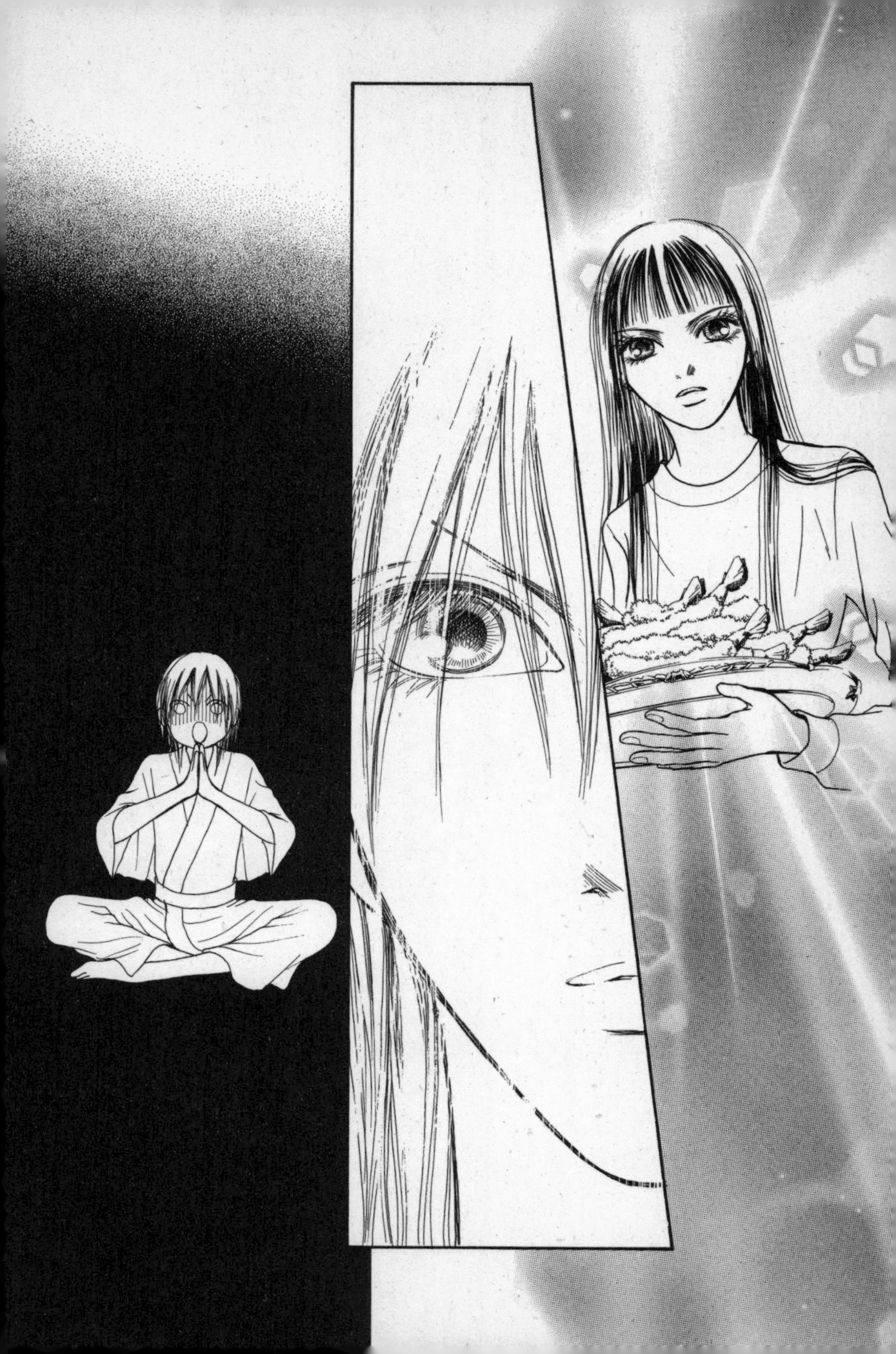

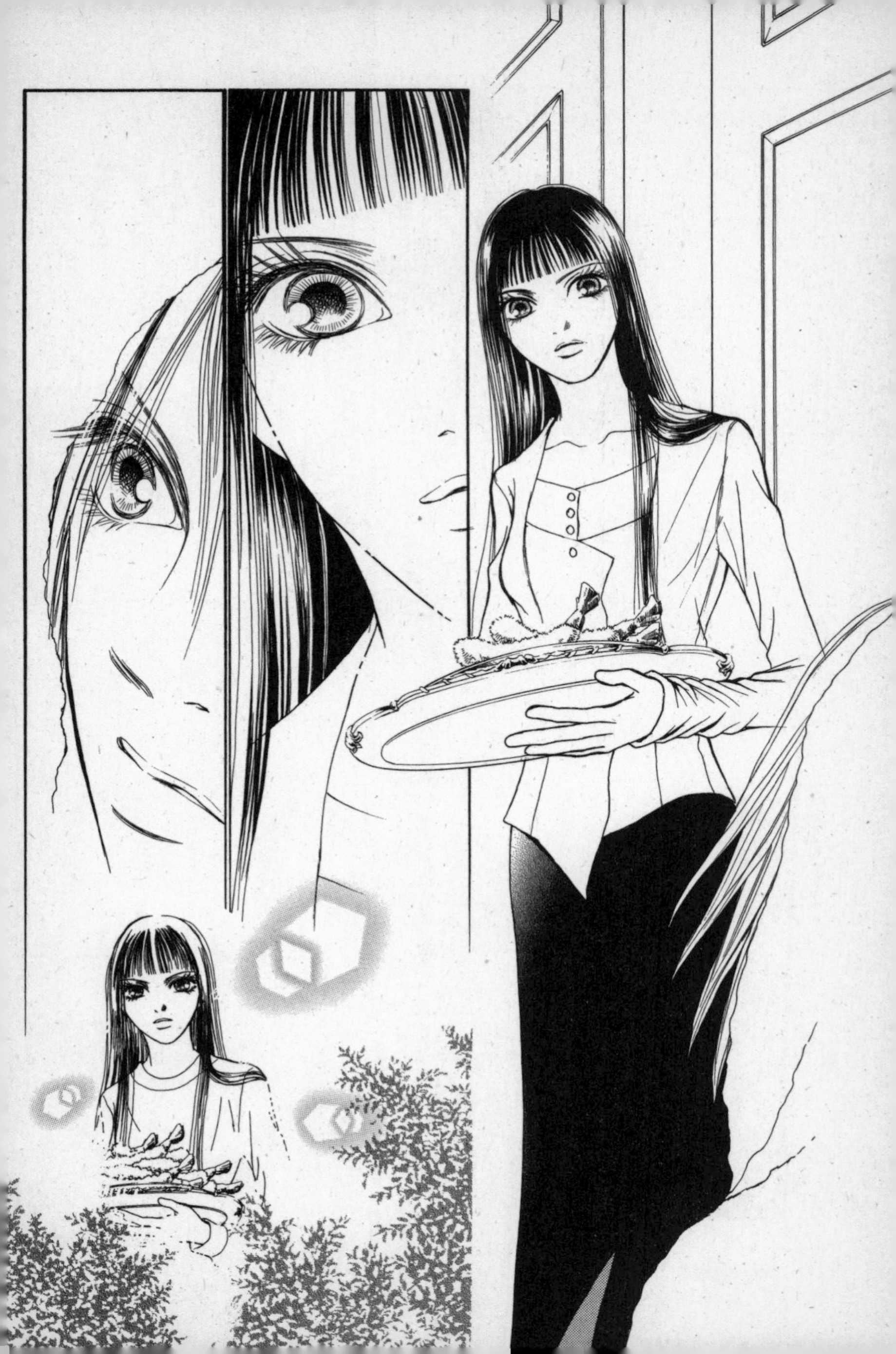

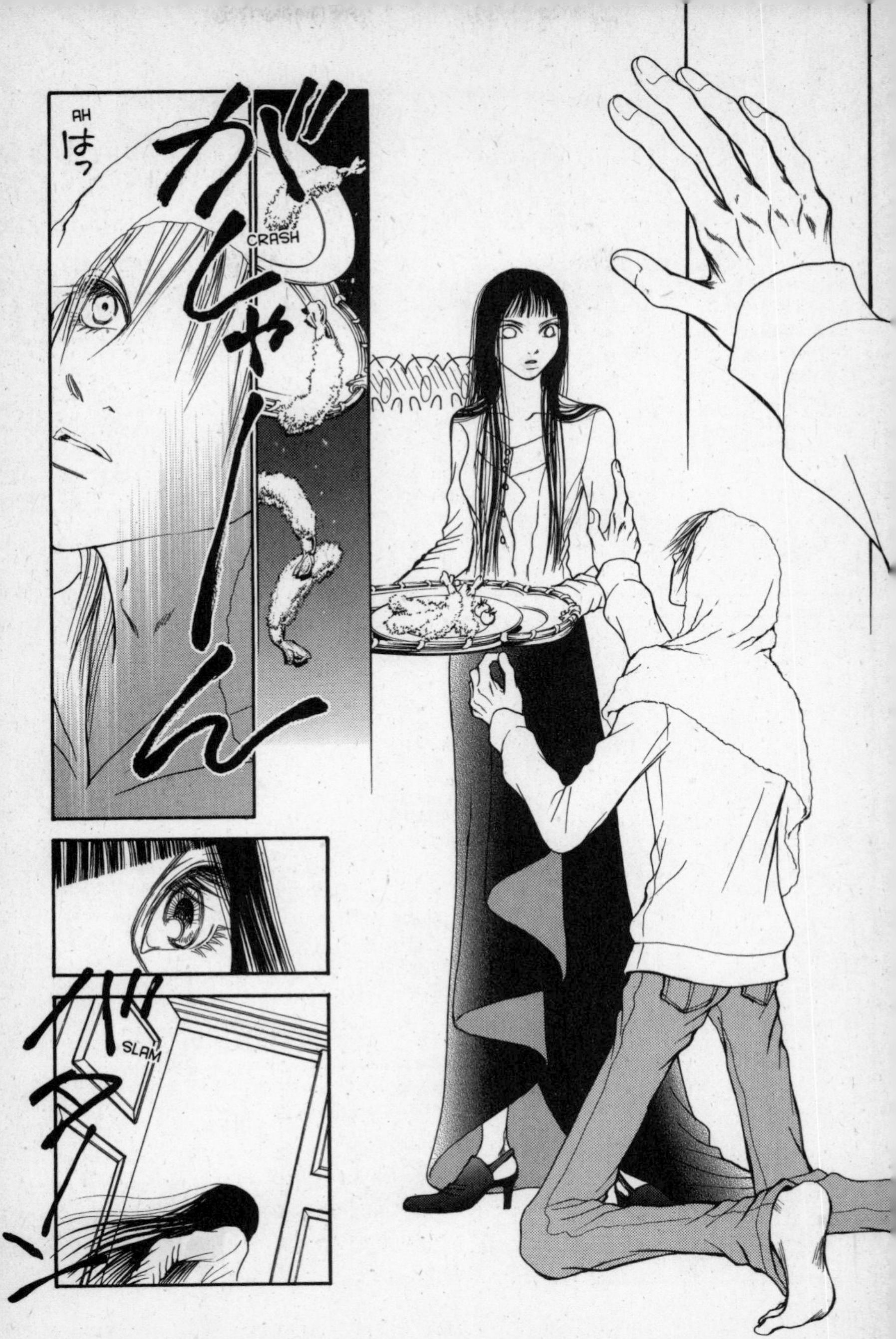
がしゃーん
CRASH
AH
はっ
バタンッ
SLAM

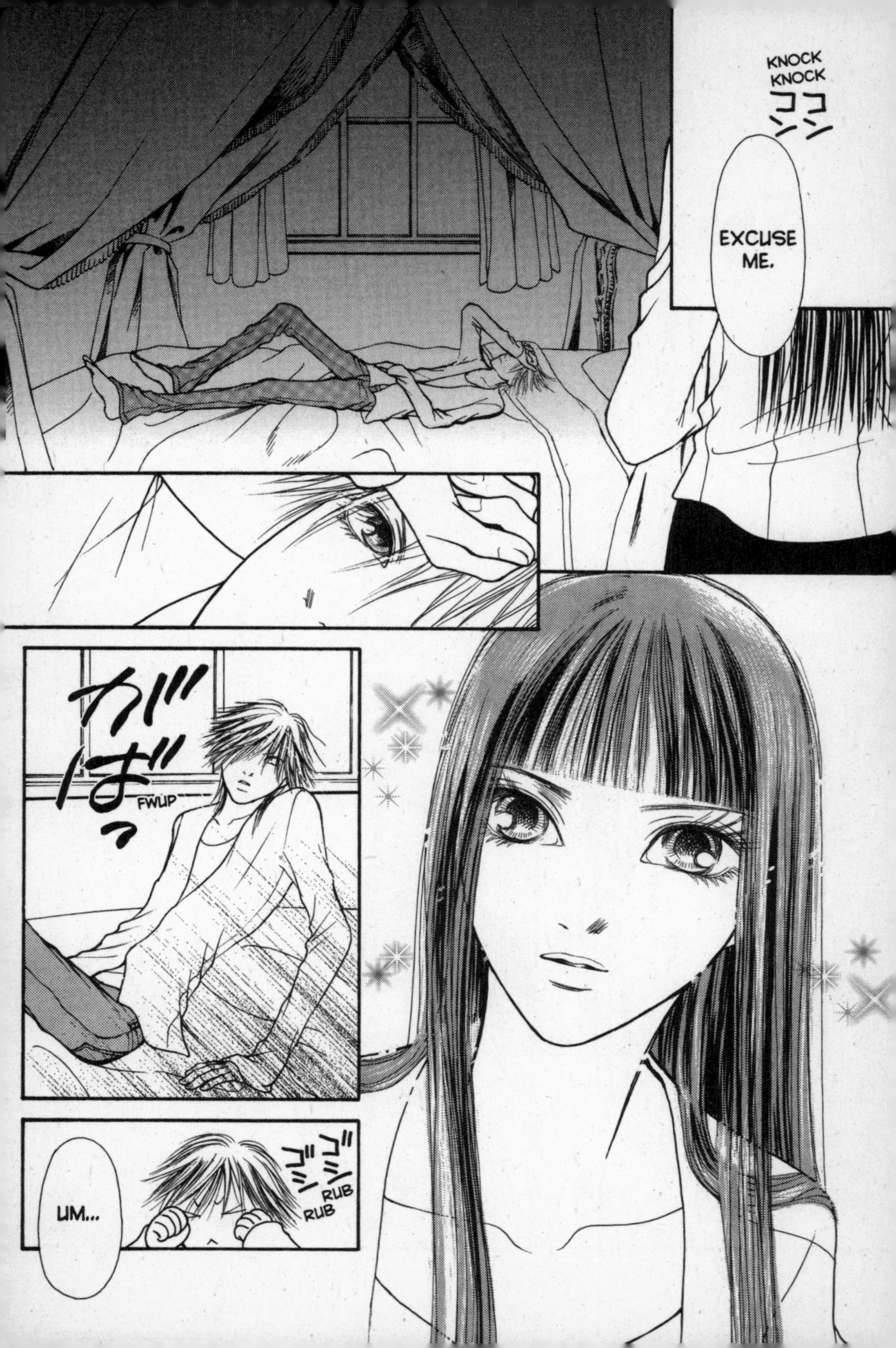
KNOCK KNOCK
コンコン
EXCUSE ME.
がばっ
FWUP
ゴシゴシ
RUB RUB
UM...

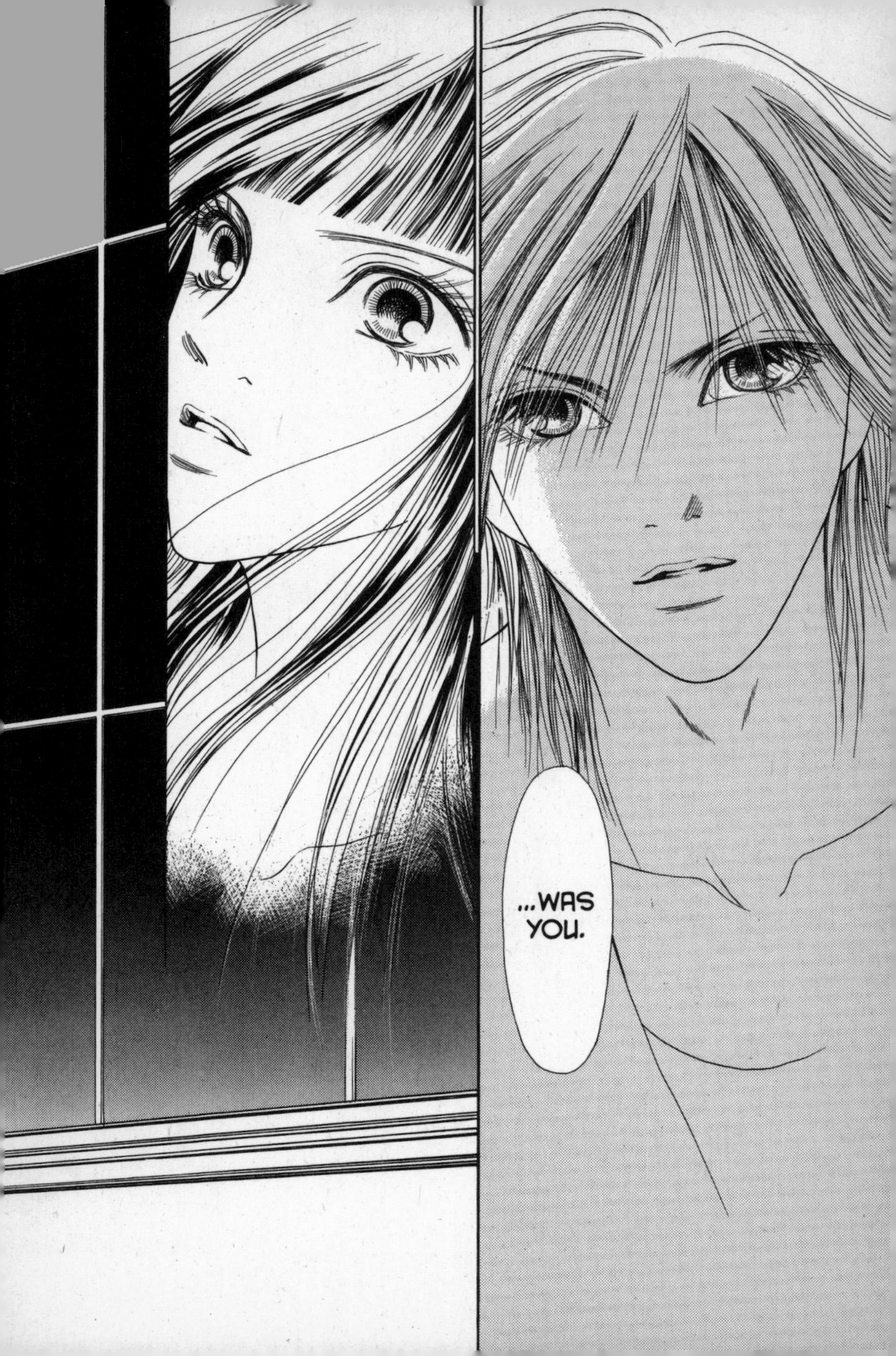
...WAS YOU.

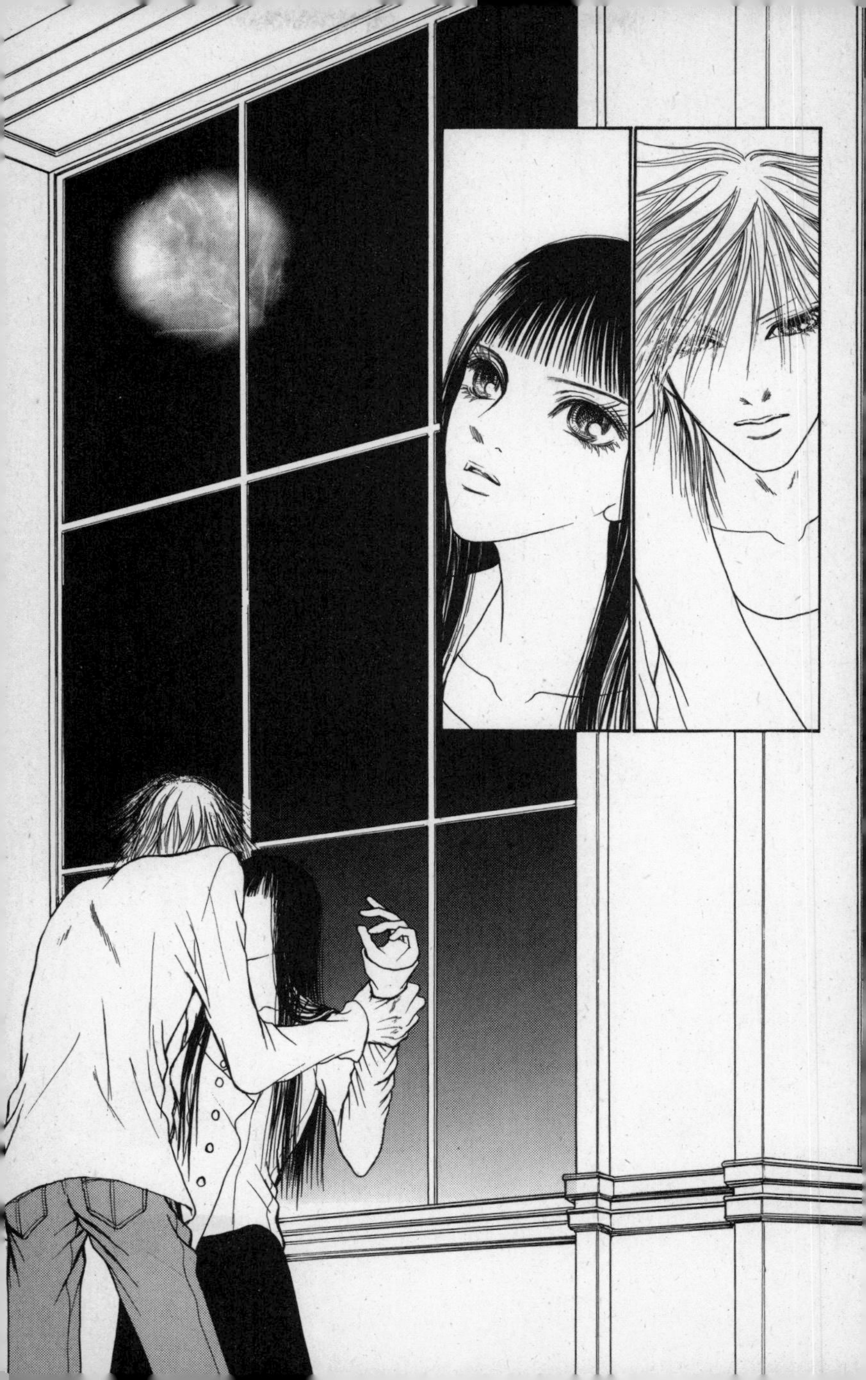

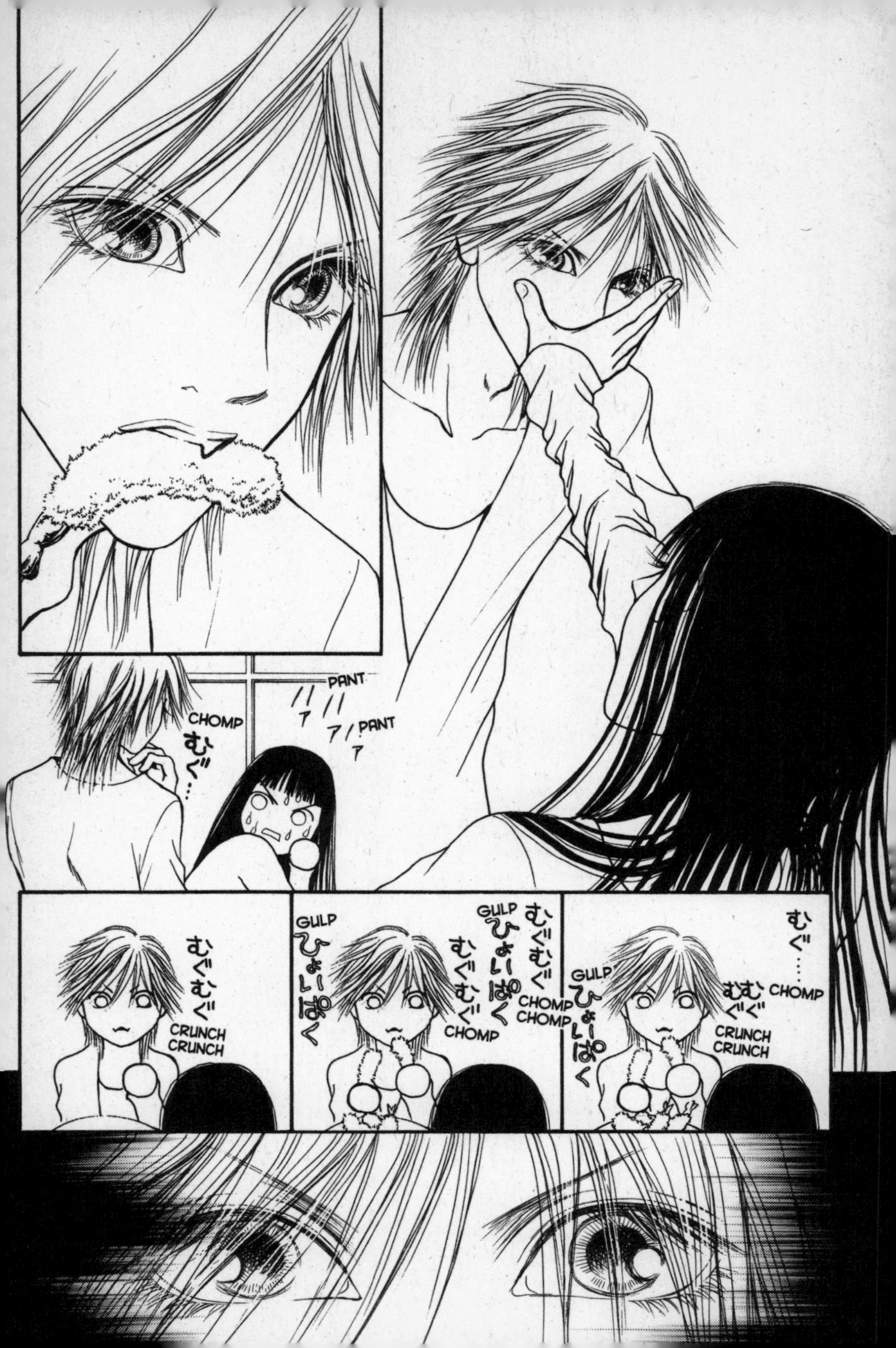

PANT
ハァ ハァ
PANT
CHOMP
むぐ…
むぐ…
CHOMP
むぐむぐ
CRUNCH CRUNCH
GULP
ひょいぱく
GULP
むぐむぐ
ひょいぱく
CHOMP CHOMP
むぐむぐ
CHOMP
GULP
ひょいぱく
むぐむぐ
CRUNCH CRUNCH

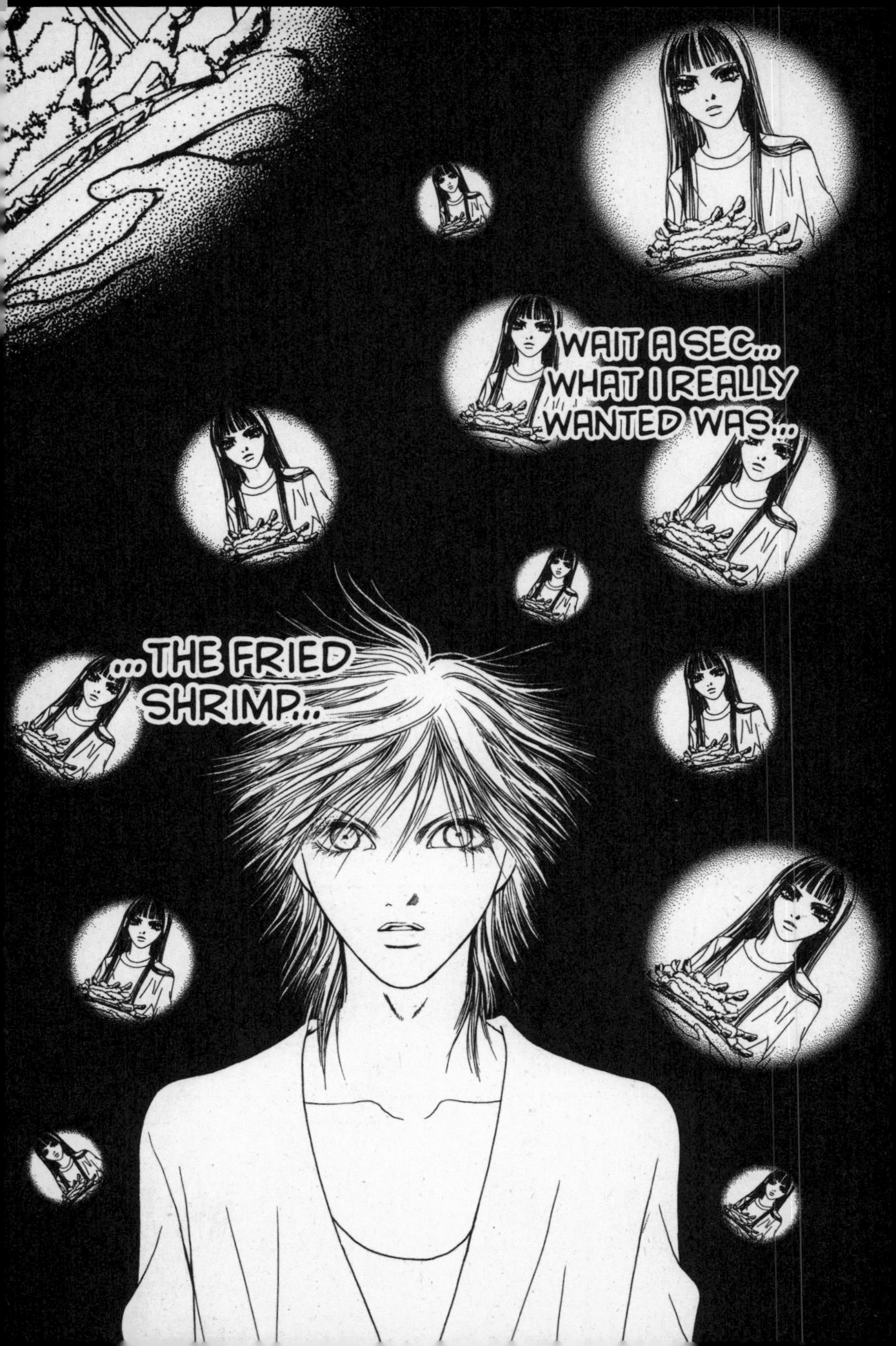
WAIT A SEC... WHAT I REALLY WANTED WAS...
...THE FRIED SHRIMP...

CONTINUED IN *WALLFLOWER* BOOK 22 ♥

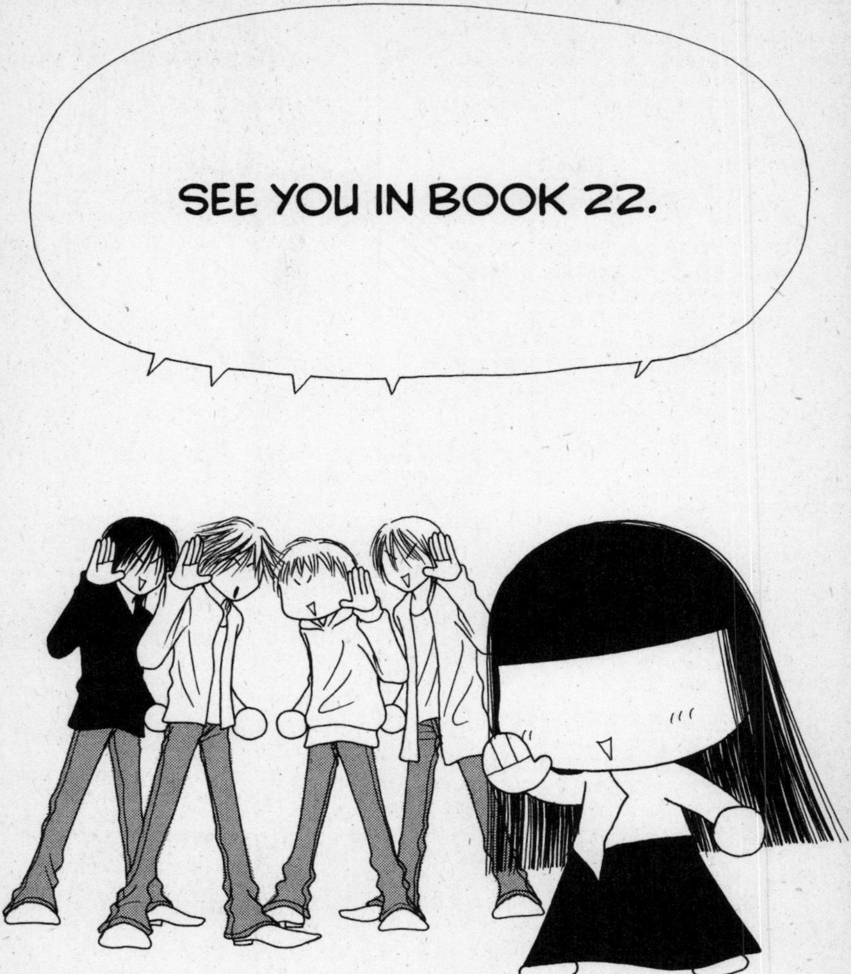
SEE YOU IN BOOK 22.

♥♥♥♥♥♥♥♥♥♥♥ I'D LIKE TO THANK YOU ALL. ♥♥♥♥♥♥♥♥♥♥♥

MY FRIEND RYON RYON (SEE THE FOLLOWING PAGE) WHO I FINALLY GOT TO CHAT WITH RECENTLY TOLD ME THAT "WHEN YOU FEEL THANKFUL, YOU SHOULD SAY IT OUT LOUD." SO I DECIDED TO TAKE THIS OPPORTUNITY TO EXPRESS MY GRATITUDE.

MERRY-SAMA

THANK YOU SO MUCH FOR WRITING SUCH BEAUTIFUL SONGS. ♡ I GET CHILLS WHENEVER I HEAR THEM, AND WHEN I HEAR THEM LIVE, THEY'RE EVEN BETTER. I'M COMPLETELY KNOCKED OUT BY YOUR BEAUTIFUL VOICE AND YOUR MELODIES.

I DON'T GO TO THEIR SHOWS AS OBSESSIVELY AS THE OTHER SIX BANDS HERE, BUT...

DIR EN GREY D'ESPAIRSRAY

I GO SEE THEM PRETTY OFTEN. THEY'RE REALLY COOL. ♡♡♡

NEW ROTE'KA-SAMA

YOU GUYS BRING ME SO MUCH PLEASURE. ♡ ♡ ♡ I WENT TO YOUR CONCERT WHEN I WAS FEELING DEPRESSED, AND BY THE END OF THE SHOW, I FORGOT ALL ABOUT MY PROBLEMS, AND I WAS FEELING GREAT. I GET ENERGIZED EVERY TIME I SEE ONE OF YOUR SHOWS. YOU MAKE ME LAUGH SO HARD. ♡ IT'S JUST SO MUCH FUN. ♡ AND THE SONGS ARE REALLY COOL. YOU GUYS'RE AMAZING! ATSU-CHAN, KATARU-KUN, NABO-CHAN, SHIZUO-SAN, I LOVE YOU GUYS. ♡♡♡♡♡

WITHOUT ALL OF YOUR CONCERTS I'D NEVER HAVE MADE IT THIS FAR IN LIFE.

KIYOHARU-SAMA

IF IT WEREN'T FOR YOU, I WOULDN'T EXIST AT ALL. I WILL BE YOUR FAN FOREVER. THE ONLY REASON KYOHEI STAYS SO HOT IS BECAUSE OF ALL THE PHEROMONES I'M SHOWERED WITH WHENEVER I GO TO YOUR CONCERTS. ♡

MITSUHIRO OIKAWA

EVERY DETAIL OF YOUR SHOW IS JUST SO AMAZING! YOUR SHOWS ARE SO VISUALLY STUNNING, THE SONGS ARE GREAT, AND IT'S JUST SO MUCH FUN. ♡ YOU'RE A TRUE STAR. WHENEVER I SEE YOU LIVE, IT MAKES ME THINK "OKAY, I'VE GOTTA WORK HARDER!" IN 2008, I WENT TO SEE MICHII TWO DAYS BEFORE MY BIRTHDAY. ♡ I HAVE A FEELING THAT I'M GONNA HAVE A FABULOUS YEAR. ♡

BOOGIEMAN-SAMA

I'M SO HAPPY TO SEE BANSAKU-SAN (FORMERLY OF BAROQUE) PLAYING BASS IN THIS BAND. I'M SUCH A BIG FAN OF YOURS!

D'ERLANGER

YOU BRING BACK MEMORIES FROM MY TEENAGE YEARS. YOU STILL SOUND AMAZING. ♡ I LOVE THE NEW SINGLE. ♡ KYO-SAN'S BAND BUG IS ALSO REALLY COOL. ♡♡♡

RYON RYON

SHE'S A VOCAL TRAINER WITH MANY STUDENTS. I'M SO THANKFUL THAT SHE FINDS TIME TO HANG OUT WITH ME. ♡ SHE'S CUTE, ♡ AND I HAVE A TON OF RESPECT FOR HER. WHEN I WAS REALLY DEPRESSED, SHE GAVE ME GREAT ADVICE THAT MADE ME FEEL SO MUCH BETTER. ♡ I'M REALLY, REALLY THANKFUL FOR THAT. ♡ ♡ ♡ I LOVE YOU SO MUCH. ♡ ♡ ♡

WRITER N-SAMA

SHE'S A POPULAR WRITER WHO ALWAYS GETS ME OUT OF THE HOUSE, AND TAKES ME TO COOL PLACES. ♡ SHE'S INTRODUCED ME TO A TON OF PEOPLE. THANKS SO MUCH. ♡ SHE HUNG OUT WITH ME ON MY BIRTHDAY IN 2008. ♡ SHE'S SUCH A BEAUTIFUL TOMBOY. ♡ I TOTALLY ADMIRE HER.

SHE WAS THE ONE WHO INTRODUCED ME TO RYON RYON. ♡

MY FRIENDS

BOTH MY FEMALE FRIENDS AND MY MALE FRIENDS...I LOVE YOU GUYS! ♡ ♡ ♡

MANGA ARTISTS I LOOK UP TO

THANK YOU SO MUCH. ♡ ♡ ♡ ESPECIALLY, MIZUHO AIMOTO-SENSEI...THANK YOU FOR EVERYTHING YOU'VE DONE FOR ME.

MY FAMILY

THANK YOU FOR YOUR KIND SUPPORT. I RESPECT AND LOVE YOU ALL. ♡ ♡ ♡ LOVE ♡ ♡

EVERYBODY WHO SENT ME LETTERS

THANK YOU SO MUCH. ♡ YOUR LETTERS ARE THE SOURCE OF MY STRENGTH. ♡ THANK YOU SO MUCH FOR READING MY MANGA. ♡

THANKS FOR READING ALL OF THIS. ♡

TENNOSUKE

LOVE 100% ♡ ♡ ♡

SORRY IT'S SO PERSONAL... AND LONG

SEE YOU IN BOOK 22. ♡

CHARACTER POPULARITY CONTEST!

I WILL NOW ANNOUNCE THE RESULTS OF THE POPULARITY CONTEST THAT WAS HELD TO COMMEMORATE THE 20TH VOLUME OF *WALLFLOWER*. BOTH MYSELF AND THE EDITING STAFF WERE ALL VERY MOVED BY YOUR POSTCARDS. I HOPE YOU'LL CONTINUE TO READ *WALLFLOWER*.

HOW COULD I LOSE TO HER?

The runner-up!

Landslide victory!

HEH... UH, HI...

The number-one horror heroine in the world of Shojo Manga!

The creature of the light was overshadowed by the darkness.

2nd PLACE
169 POINTS

TH-THANKS, EVERYBODY...

1st PLACE
239 POINTS

KYOHEI TAKANO

SUNAKO NAKAHARA

YUKINOJO TOYAMA
The cute yuki-kun appeals to women of all ages.

HOW COULD I BE IN 5TH PLACE?

TH-THANKS, EVERYBODY...

4th PLACE
70 POINTS

5th PLACE
52 POINTS

3rd PLACE
102 POINTS

RANMARU MORII
He may be a player, but girls just can't take their eyes off Ranmaru.

THANKS FOR YOUR SUPPORT.

TAKENAGA ODA
Girls will always adore the intellectual feminist Takenaga.

Voters chose their 3 favorite characters. Their top choice was awarded five points, their 2nd choice, three points and their 3rd choice, one point. The total number of points was 756.

THE RESULTS OF THE WALLFLOWER

8th PLACE
TWO-WAY TIE WITH 9 POINTS

JOSEPHINE
One of Sunako's soul mates

TAMA
The handsome ghost who followed his heart.

7th PLACE
14 POINTS

THE LANDLADY
Uber-wealthy and always in love, the landlady is the quintessential sophisticated woman.

6th PLACE
45 POINTS

NOI-CHAN
She's beautiful, sweet, a little dopey and beloved by the readers.

SUNAKO'S MOM
She's beautiful, and she looks just like Sunako(?)

10th PLACE
TWO-WAY TIE WITH 9 POINTS

A nice guy who always gets picked on.

THE KID WITH GLASSES

YUKI
Sunako's old friend. A descendant of the abominable snowwoman.

12th PLACE
TWO-WAY TIE WITH 5 POINTS

A high-class gal from a good family.

THE WEALTHY DAUGHTER

14th PLACE
4 POINTS

YAE & GIN
Yuki's beloved twin brother and sister

15th PLACE
THREE WAY TIE WITH 4 POINTS

THE FOUR LOLITAS
Devoted groupies of the four bishonen

SEBASTIAN
The landlady's butler

AKIRA
Another one of Sunako's soul mates.

THE PRINCE OF GRIMMEL
The prince of a foreign land who fell in love with Sunako

19th PLACE
4 POINTS

MACHIKO-CHAN
Yuki-kun's beloved girlfriend

OLD MAN
The wealthy daughter's butler

TSUBA-CHAN
Yuki-kun's classmate

TOMOKO HAYAKAWA
The author of Wallflower ("Not actually a character in the book)

20th PLACE
FOUR WAY TIE WITH 1 POINT

SUNAKO'S DAD
A stern father who loves his daughter

A message from Tomoko Hayakawa

Thank goodness Sunako-chan came in 1st place. I don't know what I would've done if she hadn't. I was glad to see Kyohei in 2nd too. Hang in there, Ranmaru!

I CAN'T BELIEVE HIROSHI-KUN GOT 0 POINTS. HE'S ONE OF SUNAKO'S BEST FRIENDS...

About the Creator

Tomoko Hayakawa was born on March 4.

Since her debut as a manga creator, Tomoko Hayakawa has worked on many shojo titles with the theme of romantic love—only to realize that she could write about other subjects as well. She decided to pack her newest story with the things she likes most, which led to her current, enormously popular series, *The Wallflower*.

Her favorite things are: Tim Burton's *The Nightmare Before Christmas*, Jean-Paul Gaultier, and samurai dramas on TV. Her hobbies are collecting items with skull designs and watching bishonen (beautiful boys). Her dream is to build a mansion like the one the Addams family lives in. Her favorite pastime is to lie around at home with her cat, Ten (whose full name is Tennosuke).

Her zodiac sign is Pisces, and her blood group is AB.

Translation Notes

Japanese is a tricky language for most Westerners, and translation is often more art than science. For your edification and reading pleasure, here are notes on some of the places where we could have gone in a different direction in our translation of the work, or where a Japanese cultural reference is used.

24, page 3
The American TV drama *24* is wildly popular in Japan, where a subtitled version is available on DVD.

Yakimo, page 37
Grilled sweet potatoes, called *yakimo*, are a popular treat sold by street vendors during Japan's chilly fall and winter.

Tsundere, page 37

Tsundere is an otaku term for a type of anime/manga character. It usually refers to a girl who starts out mean, and then suddenly turns sweet and lovey-dovey.

Furikake, page 61

The guys are putting *furikake* rice seasoning on top of their rice. *Furikake* is usually a blend of savory ingredients such as nori seaweed, sesame seeds, and dried fish. It is sprinkled over white rice to give it flavor.

Rabbits, page 75

It's very common for Japanese schools to keep pet rabbits on the grounds, particularly in elementary schools. Students are put in charge of caring for the rabbits.

Inside shoes, page 101

In Japanese schools, each student has a special pair of shoes used for walking inside the school.

Octopus ears, page 114

Perhaps you're wondering why Kyohei has octopi in his ears. The Japanese phrase, "mimi ni tako," literally means "calluses on the ears" and means that one has heard something so much that their ears are getting callused. However, the word for calluses, "tako," also means octopus. Hence the visual pun of octopi clinging to Sunako's ears.

Preview of Volume 22

We're pleased to present you a preview from volume 22. Please check our website (www.delreymanga.com) to see when this volume will be available in English. For now you'll have to make do with Japanese!

Papillon

BY MIWA UEDA

BUTTERFLY, SPREAD YOUR WINGS!

Ageha is a shy tomboy, but her twin sister Hana is the ultimate ultra-glam teen queen. Hana loves being the center of attention so much that she'll do anything to keep Ageha in her shadow. But Ageha has a plan that will change her life forever and no one, not even Hana, can hold her back. . . .

• From the creator of *Peach Girl*

Special extras in each volume! Read them all!

VISIT WWW.DELREYMANGA.COM TO:
• Read sample pages
• View release date calendars for upcoming volumes
• Sign up for Del Rey's free manga e-newsletter
• Find out the latest about new Del Rey Manga series

RATING T AGES 13+

The Otaku's Choice.™

GAKUEN PRINCE

BY JUN YUZUKI

CRAZY FOR COEDUCATION!

Joshi High is an elite school that most girls in Japan only dream of attending. Then one day everything changes—the all-girl school goes coed. There's just one catch: The girls outnumber the boys. So begins a wild, no-holds-barred competition for the boys of the school. Which smart and independent-minded girl will rise above the fray?

Available anywhere books or comics are sold!

TOMARE!

止まれ

[STOP!]

You're going the wrong way!

Manga is a completely different type of reading experience.

To start at the *beginning*, go to the *end*!

That's right! Authentic manga is read the traditional Japanese way—from right to left. Exactly the *opposite* of how American books are read. It's easy to follow: Just go to the other end of the book, and read each page—and each panel—from right side to left side, starting at the top right. Now you're experiencing manga as it was meant to be!